AFTER THE AMBUSH

ISBN 1-58930-018-1
Library of Congress Catalog Card Number: 2001086312

Cover Art by Norm Bergsma

Cover Design by Josh Jackson

AFTER THE AMBUSH

CHUCK DEAN

Table of Contents

Section 3

Foreword

It has been a long time since I was in Vietnam. Even though God has taken away the hurt and guilt of many of my experiences, He did not take away the memories. I believe this is because if the past is the best indicator of the future, these are lessons we need to be sharing to extend His kingdom work.

When we were in Vietnam we were not there for some higher calling, politically or otherwise. Except for our mothers, and other family members, it sure seemed like no one really cared whether we lived or died. Because all we had was each other we developed a certain kind of love relationship that humans do in times of war, and the sacrifices that we made daily were extraordinary.

On the Billy Graham Radio Program not long ago I shared what Memorial Day memories meant to me, and I think it has a lot to do with the intent of this book.

I shared this: "One day we were on a sweep and were keeping our distance. We had an observer along and he kept coming into the sweep team to ask questions, which was very disruptive to the mission. Our twenty-year old platoon sergeant kept moving in and out trying to keep the 2nd lieutenant from distracting the team. He was afraid this ignorant observer would get his men killed. The sergeant was not having much success and as the lieutenant moved towards me, the sergeant yelled to tell me to get him away from the team, and just as I turned around, Holly, our sergeant, stepped on a mine and was killed. He had become so preoccupied with the situation he did not see the obvious signs." Could we have prevented his death? I don't know, but he gave his life trying to protect ours.

After The Ambush

What spiritual implications do experiences like this have for us as Christians today? I believe when we lose sight of the signs all around us due to the pressures of everyday life, and if we are still affected by the past, we will continue to get ambushed. We must get our eyes on Jesus. For many of us we look back and realize how sad it was that we knew *about* Jesus, but we did not know Him. Now is the time to redeem those experiences for the Lord.

Instead of asking ourselves all the questions about why this happened? Or how could I have made a difference? Or why was it he and not I? We need to re-focus on Jesus and move ahead. As Christian veterans we know there is no single right answer except—Jesus. He is our Point Man, and I challenge you to allow Him to lead you through this book, applying the information for a better walk with him.

—Dana Morgan, Executive Officer, Point Man
International Ministries

Introduction

"…One point about myself, that may or may not be associated with PTSD, seems to be my uncanny knack to 'self-sabotage' most relationships I've been involved in since I 'came home' from the 'Nam.

I've been diagnosed as being 'Bi-Polar' so that may have more to do with it than simply stating, 'PTSD did it to me'. I only know that most of the time I stop myself from getting too deeply involved with any one person for too long because of the uncomfortable feelings I get inside of me.

I know myself better than anyone, so I can safely say that once I begin feeling 'Comfortable; or, 'Easy' around a person, my inner-self sets off an alarm warning me. It tells me that this too is a person too that I will eventually step over someday, and continue to march on…just like I did in 'Nam when guys were getting wasted. Then I start to isolate myself from them so that I won't have to grieve over yet another human being. Call that whatever you may, it has become a part of my inner self over time, and at times, it really sucks, Big Time. I usually hate myself for doing it but…there it is. Once I've done it I've already lost how to correct myself, and I know there's no way to back up time."
—A Vietnam Veteran in the 21ˢᵗ Century

What happened to America's veterans?

When U.S. forces went to Southeast Asia to fight in the Vietnam War during the 60's and 70's, and then again in the Persian Gulf in the 90's, most sacrificed mind, soul, emotions, and even life or limb because this country asked them to. But what has happened since coming home?

After The Ambush

I was a part of that contingency and was as convinced as everyone else that we were going to fight communist aggression, and/or control-hungry political leaders who were bent on subduing a weaker people. We were trained to fight an enemy such as the Viet Cong and North Vietnamese Army (NVA), or the Red Brigade in Iraq. We were shown photos of these soldiers and knew what they looked like before we ever engaged them in combat. We jungle-trained, and desert-trained and learned how to better survive a guerrilla war in the tropics, or the stifling heat and filth of a desert war. In spite of all this we were not prepared in any way to meet man's oldest enemy. We were not ready to engage unseen forces on the spiritual battlefields of these third-world countries. Instead we stumbled around as teenage warriors in the midst of an ancient Mecca of tribal warfare. This is a place where spiritual forces (demons) have much power over the people. Like being infected with a fast-spreading disease we became contaminated, and then came home to America with so many problems that traditional institutions were perplexed and overwhelmed about what to do. We became an enigma, a stereotype of "insanity", and a people-group who had become dangerously too complex for most civilized solutions. Even America's Christian community seemed to steer clear of dealing with us.

What happened to us?

We went to Vietnam as innocent kids to serve our military. We were half-way around the world, and during this tour of duty in 'Nam most of us unknowingly committed ourselves blindly to unseen forces. The negative fruit of our service continues to show up in different forms. The professionals have given this malady a label known as Post-Traumatic Stress Disorder (PTSD), which still continues to plague most veterans even to this day.

In the book, Nam Vet - Making Peace With Your Past, I compiled and wrote a common sense explanation of PTSD. In that work I suggested ways for veterans to begin to heal from the unwanted effects of that war. I made the observation and claimed that PTSD will not be put into remission until peace is made with God, and the only way to God the Father is by having a personal relationship with His Son, Jesus Christ. Becoming a Christ-committed Christian is the first step a person can take in making peace with his past—it is the most critical step to take in acquiring lasting healing of the harmful effects of war. For this wonderful opportunity we give our Lord God in heaven all the glory.

As I travel and meet Christian veterans it becomes more and more apparent that there is a dire need for the information in this book to be disseminated widely. Here I have attempted to bring this data into the light more because my earlier book Nam Vet: Making Peace With Your Past did not cover the topic of spiritual attack on the soldiers' souls. It is information I chose not to share in that book because my audience was primarily those who have no saving knowledge of Jesus. However, now it is time for us as Christ's soldiers to not only read and use this information, but to pass it on so the Church can begin to help the veterans in their own congregations and communities.

So what happened to us?

Clearly many Christian Vietnam veterans continue to suffer from PTSD today. Many thousands are still living defeated lives because of the ungodly spiritual baggage they carried home from S.E. Asia. I know, you will say, "But Christians cannot possibly be possessed by demons because they are indwelt with God's Holy Spirit". That's right we are indwelt with the Holy Spirit, but what difference does it make what one calls it...possessed, harassed, obsessed, etc.? If the devil has sent his demons to inflict pain and misery upon a Christian, then we must treat it the same way Jesus did...He took authority over them and commanded them to be bound and cast out!

An argument that a Christian cannot be possessed is likened to this: If someone has a gun stuck in your ribs, or if he is standing across the room pointing the gun at you, if he pulls the trigger you are still dead. The bullet has the same effect from point blank or many yards away. So it makes little difference if a demon is inside or outside, he still needs to be dealt with to alleviate problems.

After witnessing and participating in a few hair-raising deliverance prayer sessions where (Christian) veterans were set free from powerful Asian demons, I knew something had to be said about the unseen forces we stuffed in our duffle bags and brought home with us. I knew we needed to shine the light into the dark corners and flush out the enemy—the enemy that the Cross of Christ defeated a long time ago. We need to stand up and claim our dominion as sons of the Most High God!

After a few of these deliverance sessions I sought deeper into the Word of God for answers, and decided to do more in-depth research on the spiritual repercussions and aspects of the war in Vietnam. If veterans weren't getting healed and set free from the symptoms of PTSD by turning to God, then what was the solution?

I know that disobedience to God has everything to do with Satan's ability to attack and defeat us, and we cannot even resist the devil until we have submitted our lives to God ("*Submit yourselves therefore to God. Resist the devil and he will flee from you*" James 4:7). However, myself and many Point Man vets realized that there was more that needed to be known about the spiritual assaults that our veterans unknowingly went through in S.E. Asia. We needed to find out more and we needed to teach others about it before we could fight the "good fight" and begin to live in true peace and victory as Christian soldiers.

It is our prayer that you find this information a useful part of your arsenal against the enemy. It is by no means an exhaustive treatment of the subject, and our research is continually ongoing. Some of the information here is documented, and some is strictly word-of-mouth. We present it all to you for prayer. We hope you will use it in your ministry to help our veterans and their families to free themselves in a world and country that has been ambushed by the chief conspirator of all ... Satan. These are lessons we have paid a heavy price to learn—we now offer them to you free of charge. The men and women of Point Man Ministries believe what is written here can assist you and your loved ones in making it safely out of the ambush's "kill zone". Be prepared for a good fight though—the enemy doesn't want to give up this ground easily.

Section 1

Chapter One

The Ambush

THE SECULAR WAY OF BRINGING MENTAL HEALTH AND HEALING TO the Vietnam veteran continues to produce sporadic and impermanent results. It has since the war in Vietnam ended. One veteran described the traditional institutional therapy and practices are like "putting band-aids on bullet holes." The bleeding just gets covered up with drugs and Freudian techniques. The majority of the programs implemented by the government merely teach veterans how to "cope" with their problems. They have no permanent solutions simply because they do not understand, or adhere to, the Biblical truths regarding the spiritual makeup of man. They know little about the spiritual enemies that battle for the souls of men on a daily basis.

To understand what really happened to our troops in S.E. Asia, and why some are seemingly hopeless cases, with "incurable" stress problems, it is most important to look from the spiritual perspective. We must look at the eternal, not the physical.

Before the United States entered this war in Vietnam, France had been occupying the country for many years. France failed to keep peace between the warring tribes of Vietnam and were ousted: History reveals that in the areas of Vietnam, Laos, Cambodia, and Thailand there have been century old battles between these tribes.

During that time much of the religion in these areas was Buddhism or Hinduism mixed with Spiritism (worshiping ancestral spirits). Over the centuries this part of the world has been given over to pagan spiritual powers, (see Ephesians 6:10-11-12.) When the tribes went to war with one another they called on their gods (rulers and powers) and spirits to fight for them. During these battles they learned how to call on spirits to destroy their opponents. When foreign powers came to their countries they did no different. They used these same spiritual forces against them. Our American military went to fight a physical war, not a spiritual one, and were spiritually ambushed. Much sickness, confusion, mental torment, and death (especially through suicide) followed.

Spirits Dominate the Tribes

In an effort to make peace, and be friendly with the peoples of S.E. Asia whom they were sent to protect, many young Americans participated in rituals and customs of foreign gods, and consequently fell under their evil powers. The tribes of S.E. Asia already knew of these powers and had yielded to them as their forbearers had done for centuries. Our young exuberant soldiers had no idea of what they were inviting into their lives, and the curses and demonic possession swept them away.

The following is an excerpt from the January, 1965 issue of <u>National Geographic</u> magazine. It gives witness to our observations and research. Captain Gillespie, U.S. Army Special Forces, is the article's principal subject. He was assigned to a mountain tribe as a military advisor during the war:

> "I overheard Gillespie, his right hand now on Y Jhon's shoulder, say, 'I want no troops moved out of this camp until I say so, Y Jhon.' Head bowed, Y Jhon moved a few paces off, then returned. In his fractured English he explained that he had just thought

of a plan to keep the Vietnamese (suspected Viet Cong) in the camp from harm at the hands of his Montagnards. He and Gillespie...who were already blood brothers in the Rhade tribe...would undergo a ceremony of alliance with Captain Truong and invoke the protection of the spirits. Gillespie agreed and Y Jhon hurried away to alert his sorcerer.

"For the mountain people, life is dominated by an endless number of spirits that rule the fate of men and animals, control the elements, and govern the harvest. These spirits must be cultivated and placated through sacrifices. The sorcerer, who possesses high status and great influence, deals directly with the spirits. To appease them, the Montagnard may progressively offer a chicken, then a pig, finally a buffalo. Sometimes these sacrifices deplete the entire livestock population of a village.

"So, in his difficulty, Y Jhon had turned naturally to the spirits. If he became allied to both Captain Gillespie and Captain Truong, he could not move against them, kill them, or harm them; at the same time, they would protect him. A simple solution for a simple man. At a time like this, I thought, a lesser man than Gillespie would not have realized the necessity of, or taken the time for, the ceremony. Gillespie's understanding may have been the decisive factor in keeping control of Y Jhon and the camp."

It appears here that Gillespie was the one who was victorious in this volatile situation because he had enough "insight" to yield to a demonic ceremony, and that his superior command of diplomacy saved the day. But, I submit this to you. Who really won? I believe the power demon that controlled the entire village won the victory by implanting evil spirits into another American. I wonder how Captain Gillespie is doing these days? Does he have nightmares? A drinking problem? Thoughts of suicide? Has he escaped the demonic wars unscathed? I wonder. He certainly needs our prayers in any case.

The Ceremony

This is a continuation from the January 1965 <u>National Geographic</u> article that so aptly describes the demonic influence on Americans during the war in S.E. Asia.

> "Shortly after 10:00 a.m. we walked to the ceremonial hut. Huge brass gongs announced the arrival of the sorcerer, a sunken-faced man with watery eyes. A delegation of camp and village dignitaries faced a row of seven jars, each brimful of fermented rice mash and water—a potent concoction. Food offerings lay beside the jars: one pig and a chicken as an offering for Gillespie, a chicken each for Y Jhon, Captain Truong, and the sorcerer. Chanting, the sorcerer communicated with the spirits. After each communication the participants sipped rice beer.
>
> "The climax of the ceremony came when the sorcerer, after one particularly long draught of brew, crouched alongside Captain Gillespie and fastened a draught ring to his right wrist. This…joining a twin ring from the previous ritual that had united Gillespie and Y Jhon…would give notice to the spirits that a suitable offering had been made."

I remind you; this is not from a charismatic Christian publication, it is from a 1965 National Geographic magazine. Isn't it more than just a little odd that even a secular publication could report on the obvious demonic aspects of the war in Vietnam on such a broad scale, and yet the Church in America remained so blind to it for so long?

Chapter Two

Curses

MOST ALL SYMPTOMS OF POST-TRAUMATIC STRESS DISORDER THAT plagues hundreds of thousands of Vietnam veterans today, are of a spiritual nature—and a bi-product of pagan curses. They can be brought under control by means of the spiritual warfare God has defined and outlined in the Holy Scriptures. (See Section II "After the Ambush" for in-depth information on this warfare.)

In late 1989 when I worked at Point Man Ministries' headquarters we received a verbal report that an ex-Buddhist monk had shared some vital information with an American pastor regarding demonic curses being cast upon American troops during the Vietnam War. When we heard this it was as though a curtain had been pulled up for us. We started getting a glimpse of the unseen war that we had been subjected to and how it still affected us and other veterans.

We saw that Satan's playground and battlefield is mostly in the minds of men, and we began to take serious notice of how these so-called curses may had affected all Vietnam veterans. When we did, we realized that Post-Traumatic Stress Disorder's origin had more of an explanation than simply being beaten down by the rigors of combat of an unpopular war and being spit upon when we got home. The unseen enemy had ambushed us!

After The Ambush

According to this ex-Buddhist priest an entire sect of Vietnamese Buddhist monks spent years heaping curses on all Americans that came to fight in their country. These specific curses were:

1. That the American soldiers would become wandering men for the rest of their lives.
2. That they would never find peace.
3. That they would be angry men and women for the rest of their lives.

When we heard this we realized that these curses epitomized the lives of many veterans, and we knew we had to learn more.

What happened to our men and women? They were ambushed by the devil. The spirits and curses of the land and pagan religions attached themselves to our soldiers and began to torment them mentally through flashbacks, nightmares, suicide, drugs, alcohol, alienation, isolation, anger, rage, depression, and numbness of feelings.

These Americans became wounded souls. They then brought this torment back to live with them in their homes, families, and their social relationships. They had been deeply wounded by an elusive enemy in the spirit realm. Sadly most American clergy did not recognize it as a "spiritual" problem and some readily accepted Freudian-type solutions. Consequently the church has had no answers to the ceaseless agony of the Vietnam veteran.

The American church has relegated the matter of post-war stress to the secular field of psychiatry. They turned it over to man, instead of God. Secular doctors have concluded that Post-Traumatic Stress Disorder is incurable, and sadly most veterans have bought this bill of goods and are depressed because of it. The reason for that conclusion is simply this; the natural man does not know how to bring spiritual deliverance to the souls of men. As ministers of Jesus Christ we know how—it is all written in God's Word. The time is past due to reach out to the Vietnam veteran through eternal eyes. It is now time to help them get free from the bondage of a covert enemy, and it is time to truly welcome them home in the Lord.

Chapter Three

Allowing The Enemy Entrance

Prostitution

THROUGHOUT HISTORY WHEREVER YOU FIND AN ARMY YOU ALSO find prostitutes. When I first arrived in Vietnam in 1965 a "short-time" girl cost approximately 78 cents. I understand that inflation caught up with things over the years between 1965 and 1973, and a "short-time" was up to 4 or 5 dollars in some places. Only a few soldiers did not frequent the prostitutes. Many pimps, with his contingent of girls, would actually follow some American units out on patrol to make paid-for sex available even in dangerous zones. It was an enterprising business, and one that had devastating effects on the young troops who partook.

The Bible states clearly that two become one flesh when they participate in the sex act. Spiritual bonding and ungodly transferences occur during the sex act, and many things are passed between two people when engaged in illicit sex.

It is a point of interest that ceramic nick-knacks made in the Orient have holes in the bottom of them. These are placed there to allow the spirits free access to come and go as they please. Also it is worthy to note that the Montagnard soldiers (mountain people) about to go into battle would always smear their mouths and under their noses with a mixture of mint, etc. to keep evil spirits from entering them through open orifices on the battlefields. This was to keep the spirits of the dead soldiers from entering into them.

In Asia it is an accepted belief that spirits enter and leave from the orifices of the body. *All the orifices!*

As the thousands of Americans copulated and entered S.E. Asian women they opened themselves to a bonding union that gave free access for spirits to enter them. In this act there were also exchanged the feelings of anger, hatred, revenge, rape, repressed murder, despair, and homesickness, all building up for a temporary release in the sex act, drugs and alcohol. (It is no wonder that booze is called "spirits"). Perhaps many of the problems veterans have today with family relationships can be traced to some of this ungodly bonding in a very pagan and demonic environment.

Souvenirs.

As curious and sentimental kids most of us allowed the enemy entrance by stuffing our pockets and packs full of souvenirs (trinkets, money, charms, jewelry, etc.). Nearly every Vietnam veteran I know has some sort of war souvenir from his time in 'Nam. One particular item of importance is the Vietnamese money that many still carry around today.

One of the facial images of a demon-god from the Temple of Cao Dai can be seen in the near invisible watermark imprinted on the Hai Muoi Dong (20 Piaster) currency bill of the now non-existent South Vietnamese government. (See the drawn illustration of the demon in this watermark below).

You cannot see the horrifying face of this Cao Dai demon until you hold it up to the light, and when the light shines through you see it. When I first discovered it I thought it was a joke, but then realized that it was one of the ways I was letting the enemy have entrance into my life. I shuddered to think that I carried it around in my pocket. And as for holding it up into the light? I can think of no better representation of Satan's clandestine operating methods than this. But, praise God! Once we seek God's truth and allow His light to shine on the enemy we render him even more powerless.

Carrying a demon of Cao Dai in our pockets were real wake-up calls for the veterans involved in Point Man Ministries when we discovered it on that bill. As a result we began to research more about Cao Dai. We soon found that one of the Vietnamese interpretations of Cao Dai means "from the high places," and it is not only just a demon-god, but a strong principality over all S.E. Asia. In another interpretation Cao Dai means "the eye of God", and is exactly the same pyramid and eye configuration of the Illuminati, a powerful secret cult of western civilization. This pyramid also appears on the American one-dollar bills which millions of people carry and handle every day. I believe Cao Dai to be the "power-demon" that commands (Ephesians 6:10-11;12) lesser demon gods and evil spirits in Asia. He is the head guy for that area, and when he is rendered ineffective and cast out, the lesser demons must also leave with him. When this is done it brings much relief to the person who has been suppressed by their presence.

Chapter Four

Tet

TET IS A NATIONAL CELEBRATION OF THE LUNAR NEW YEAR, and most Vietnamese, as well as the Chinese, celebrate it through many customs and habits that have prevailed for many centuries. Most Vietnam veterans do not think of Tet as a time to celebrate, but a time that still brings chills to their souls. We hear the word and immediately think of the accelerated times of combat, terror, and loss of many friends in the tough battles which were fought around this time of the year in Vietnam. It is, however, much more significant than what we think when it comes to the spiritual battles fought for the souls of men who are wrestling with PTSD and the bad memories of this defining time in our past. Therefore, it is important to have a look at how Tet spiritually affected us all.

A few years ago a veteran who served as an American helicopter pilot in the war gave me a small pamphlet on Tet. It clearly demonstrates another way in which our troops were unwaryingly exposed to demonic activities while serving in S.E. Asia. By excerpting some important passages we see how the South Vietnamese (our allies) actually invited us to partake in their traditional worship (which was satanic in nature). Most all of us thought it was just an innocent gesture to bring us into closer unity with our allies, but instead we fell into a most subtle trap of fraternizing with the real enemy. We did it without reservation or hesitation—and we walked blindly into a spiritual ambush and never knew when we were hit.

Here is the excerpt from the pamphlet issued to American soldiers to help us join and celebrate a pagan ritual:

TET, The Vietnamese New Year

Written and prepared by Colonel Nhieu Do Kien, Headquarters, I Corps

"*Presented here are the most representative habits and customs of the Vietnamese TET. To understand the Vietnamese, and the complexities of their material and spiritual life, there is no better way than to live side by side with them, by mixing in the Vietnamese society to learn for yourself. We are sure that you will discover many other pleasant aspects of it.

"We wish you much success.

"In Vietnam, TET is not only an occasion for the Vietnamese to rest and have a good time as a compensation for the many days of toil and hardship, but it is also an opportunity for them to remember their ancestors, to maintain the latter's graves, to pay visits to relatives and neighbors to tighten the bonds of family and social relationship, and TET is a religious feast in which people express their prayers and worship for their saints, gods, and ancestors...

"Finally, because of the Vietnamese belief in Astrology according to which the life of each individual is governed by stars that change every year, TET brings hope for everybody that the change will work for the better. The ill hope for better health, the poor hope to become richer, and the wealthy hope to become more powerful...*

"Year-end celebration. At private homes, this celebration aims at worshipping the ancestors, and inviting them to join with their children and grandchildren during the TET holidays...

"Custom of Divination. The Vietnamese have another custom which is divination. They often divine in the theater. In this the plays are Chinese and are acted out for the visitors to come to divine. The people who come to divine need not watch all the play. They can watch only apart of it and from that part determine if their fortune is going to be good or bad during the coming year."

Chapter Five

Veterans Viewing Vietnam Today

RECENTLY A SECULAR VETERAN GROUP THAT IS ACTIVE IN A U.S. prison mailed me a newsletter and I took special notice of the subtle spiritual ambush in the content as I read it. It dawned on me that even though the Vietnam War has been over for decades; the effects of the devil's assault on many American veterans still prevail. This is one lesson that we Christian soldiers must be alerted to—many of our brothers and sisters from that era are still in the ambush "kill zone" and need our help.

One of the key articles written in this mailing was titled "Viewing Vietnam." This article illustrates how veterans, without the guidance of the Holy Spirit, still look at some of the aspects of life in S.E. Asia. After all these years most still have no idea that the root cause of their problems center on their spiritual, emotional, and physical connections to the pagan practices of the country they fought and lived in. Little do they know their souls were captured, and they became prisoners of a spiritual war and did not even know it.

Here is that newsletter's article:

"Animism, the belief that spirits exist in the world of animate and inanimate objects like rocks and trees, is part of the religion of many Vietnamese. It is predominately the religion of the Montagnards, the highlanders. The Animist lives in a world inhabited by spirits—both good and bad. These spirits are active in influencing the outcome of daily events.

After The Ambush

The Animist believes that he must care for the spirits to keep from angering them or causing them to re-enter the visible world. He thinks of these spirits as capable of having human emotions, and he believes that they can be greedy, deceptive, unpredictable, bitter and even revengeful. However, the spirits of men who were good while alive do not cause problems, provided that they are properly cared for by their families. Rites have to be performed to send these souls to the world of spirits in the proper manner.

While the Animist does not want to offend spirits, he also desires to use them to his advantages. Just as members of other religions that we are familiar with pray to 'go betweens' to help them ask for favors from their deity, the Animist uses spirits to help him achieve his goals in life. He engages in prayer and ritual to cause them to do his will and to placate those spirits which otherwise would harm him.

The most important man in the village of the Animist is the sorcerer. It is the sorcerer who gives advice on what the moods of the spirits are and what can be done to please him. The Animist also places a great deal of emphasis on omens, which appear in the form of dreams or even as happenings, in the real world. For example, a dog sneezing at a wedding is considered to be a sin that the wedding is a mistake, and the wedding is halted immediately. A traveler who sees the tracks of an animal across the trail may consider this to be a sign that the spirits are against him. He may stop his trip, return to the village, and consult with the sorcerer to find out how he can continue his trip.

An important concept in the life of an Animist is that the dead must be given proper burial. To deny the dead this privilege is to condemn the dead person's spirit to aimless wandering. The Animist also believes that to mutilate or decapitate the body harms the spirit as well as the body. During the Vietnam War, forces from both sides used this belief in their terrorism by decapitating those who would not submit to them or who openly opposed them.

From birth to death the world of the Animist is filled with concern for spirits. So when working with the Animists, you must take care not to offend the spirit, or you may anger your hosts.

Respect their spirits, their beliefs, and you will be showing respect for them."

During the war in Vietnam we always knew when we were being ambushed. It was there in living color, with all the terror that comes with someone trying to take your life by surprise with guns and explosives. However, as pointed out in the above newsletter the spiritual ambushes are not as easily seen or recognized. There is still much work to do if we expect to snatch our comrades from the "kill zone" in time.

Chapter Six

Ambush—The Beat Goes On

"Every time I kill someone, I get farther away from home..."
　　　　　　—Tom Hanks in "Saving Private Ryan"

As THE 90's DECADE BEGAN NEARLY 400,000 AMERICANS WERE poised on the border of Saudi Arabia and Iraq waiting for orders to attack or defend against Saddam Hussein's Red Guard. It looked like another Vietnam on the horizon. However, because of the lessons our leaders learned in the 60's and 70's in S.E. Asia, the Gulf War ended quickly and victoriously for the Allied Forces sent to the region. Within hours they put a stop to Hussein's play for power, and America was relieved that it did not become a protracted war of attrition like Vietnam was.

We were in the Gulf for what appeared to be humane reasons... "To free the oppressed." But like Vietnam there was much more at stake than protecting another people's land and property. The political and economic reasons were glaringly apparent, and for reasons of staying focused on the subject (our real enemy—Satan) we will not delve into those reasons.

For many heart-rending days American soldiers were placed in a pagan culture in the Mid-East. Many tried to find ways of adjusting to the war at hand. They did their best to be in rapport with things in that culture so as to ease the pain and anxiety of being far from home and under the stressful conditions of possible death looming in their faces. They tried to find a little bit of peace and comfort in socializing with the people they had been sent to fight for and protect.

Unlike Vietnam, our country went into a season of prayer for the soldiers and the entire situation. Prayer vigils sprung up all over the country. Thousands of churches prayed unceasingly and came against the demonic forces and curses that our military people were being bombarded with from the spirit realm. This is probably one of the single-most important lessons we learned (as a country) from the Vietnam War—during the Persian Gulf War (because of what we saw in Vietnam) we learned that we could not depend on our government to protect and care for our soldiers while in war or after...so we prayed! The results were that the war in the Gulf only lasted a matter of hours before it was under control and our people were not in harm's way. However, as we now are finding out, many of the veterans from even that short war are having problems called the Gulf War Syndrome. What happened to them?

Even though the war in the Gulf was short-lived we cannot expect their time of conflict to be any different than ours in Vietnam, and we must recognize the enemy's devices to disrupt lives, and "take their souls captive." So let's see how they were ambushed as well.

It has been documented that Saddam Hussein, the leader of Iraq, declared himself a direct descendant from King Nebuchadnezzar, and has vowed to rid the world of Jews and their allies. At the time of the Gulf War the ancient city of Babylon (in Iraq) was under reconstruction for several years. Saddam had spent millions of dollars on its erection.

Many end time signs abounded through the whole crisis in the Middle East, but I believe we need to look back through some basic Bible history to see an important part of the real threat that our forces were faced with there.

Geographically where were our young soldiers? Historically we see that the Garden of Eden was located somewhere near the intersection of the Tigris and Euphrates Rivers, which happens to be in northern Iraq. Sin was first introduced to mankind in that very location, so evil found it's inaugural roots in Iraq! As far as we know our military was completely unaware that our men and women were so close the very mouth of Satan's lair, and most believed that their war was against flesh and blood. They came home influenced by the spirit realm, and most cannot understand why they have problems with their family life and other relational problems that are similar to those still plaguing many Vietnam veterans. But we know, and it is our responsibility to lead the way as point men for Christ—He is their only deliverer.

The Gulf War, the conflict in Kosovo, and all the future military engagements that our men and women will find themselves fighting in will never be void of spiritual implications. We know that this world will always have wars—right to the end, ("And you will be hearing of wars and rumors of wars; see that you are not frightened, for those things must take place..." Matthew 24:6). We cannot count on peace, nor can we count on our governmental institutions to address the spiritual issues and problems that impact soldiers during combat. It is our charge as responsible Christian veterans to listen to the winds of the Spirit to lead us into the ministry of compassion, understanding and love for those who will seek us out for help. It is by our experiences that they will identify us, and it is with our healing prayers on their behalf that we will achieve eternal success and bring them all the way home.

As Christian soldiers we know that it is our duty to prepare ourselves and others for the spiritual battlefields ahead. We have been given this assignment and now walk by faith—not by sight. Welcome to the war.

Section 2

Chapter Seven

We Few, We Faithful Few

*"For day by day men came to David to help
him, until there was a great army like the army of
God"*
(1 Chronicles 12:22).

IN EVERY WAR THERE ARE ALWAYS A FEW GOOD MEN AND WOMEN chosen to fight and disrupt enemy activities and set captives free.

Not long ago I had the honor of speaking with one of the WWII infantrymen who discovered the German concentration camp at Dakau, and liberated the Jews imprisoned there. What a sense of accomplishment and pride I sensed in him as he spoke. As a soldier this one event highlighted his entire war experience. With tears of compassion, and memories of horrifying scenes of half-dead prisoners left by the Nazi's, he spoke clearly and very detailed of what he went through. He mentioned that in all that evil, he felt that he had been chosen to be there to set those people free. There was no doubt he would risk his life again today to do the same if the situation presented itself. In God's army there are soldiers chosen to risk everything as well. They become servants willing to survive on little, and go wherever the Commander leads. Their mission is to take the gospel of Christ to the lost and dying, and to rescue prisoners of war from the dark confines of P.O.W. camps. (*"The Spirit of the Lord is upon me, because he has anointed me to preach the gospel to the poor; he has sent me to proclaim release to the captives, and recovery of sight to the blind, to set free those who are downtrodden, to proclaim the favorable year of the Lord"* Luke 4:18.)

God's soldiers *know* there is a war raging, and do something about it.

And as for war, we live in a world at war. It is unavoidable. If it isn't "hot war" it is "cold war." There is mounting tension between different nations, races and ideologies. Even in the privacy of our homes we find no refuge. It seems that we are constantly dealing with problems that cause strife between husband and wife, between parents and children. The enemy is focusing on Christian families like never before, and today there are millions of veterans leading these family units. What hope can we give them? This section is designed to impart the confidence needed to bring victory and freedom for one of God's most precious and powerful weapons—the family.

The Christian Life Means War

As the Bible teaches many will come as false teachers and prophets to deceive "even the elect." Our foe is even using the Word of God in the hands of charlatans to tear Christian marriages and families apart. It is sad, and in these last days people around the world search in vain for a way out.

An army drill instructor once said to a trainee, "Your platoon is almost surrounded, and you are running out of ammunition. As platoon commander, what steps would you take?"

"Long ones, sergeant," the new soldier replied.

The only problem with that thinking is that in spiritual warfare you cannot run from it. If you ignore it or try to hide from it, it will only engulf you more.

44

Man has been surrounded since the fall of Adam and Eve, and can't seem to take steps long enough to escape the on-slaught of an enemy bent on taking him to hell. Whether he is aware of it or not, he is in a spiritual trap like a hunted animal, and is a participant in the oldest war of all time. Had it not been for the work done on the cross of Calvary by Jesus Christ, there would be no hope whatsoever of having eternal freedom. Enlisting to serve in God's Army is a conscious choice each soldier must make to break through the ambush to a life of eternal security. Sadly enough many will not make it to the other side.

Humans are at war with humans because humans are at war with God. Behind the human battle there is a spiritual battle. It is the age-old fight between darkness and light, between good and evil, between God's children and Satan. Neutrality is virtually impossible. Each human is on one side or the other; not one of us can remain in a "no man's land" and claim to be unaffected by the war around us.

The Christian life means warfare. The battlefield, the weapons, and the foe are all spiritual rather than material. When you decide to answer the call to Christ's service you will find that you cannot ignore "the acts of war" that take place on earth as well as the heavenlies. You will be required to know about this war, and called upon by the Supreme Commander to walk strongly by His Spirit, and obey His commands. You will also have assignments designed (through Him) to set the captives free. This section focuses on helping you develop the required soldierly functions to endure every "good fight"—and gain victory in the name of Jesus Christ.

What are God's Soldiers Like?

There are two kinds of Christian soldiers: one who joins the army and slides through pay-check to pay-check, and the other who goes to war. One soldier actively engages the enemy, using God-given authority, and faithfully hones his combat skills for daily service. The other has false notions that there is no war going on at all. He flirts with the world and accepts its lies. He doubts and has unbelief about spiritual enemies and may even harbor an attitude that Satan is a doctrinal myth. This kind of Christian is a serious liability to God's plan in wrestling the "prisoners of war" from the chains of the devil. Sadly enough, a large portion of the church now falls into this category.

The soldiers in God's Army are made up of ministers, missionaries, and every born-again Christian who tries to walk out the Great Commission (Matthew 28:19). Schooled and trained to be salt and light to a dying world, we have been sent as emissaries of the church for hundreds of years. As history reveals many are sent on assignments ill-equipped to stand against the schemes of Satan—and soon become ineffective casualties of war. This happens because they were not told about, or refused to heed, the biblical warnings regarding spiritual warfare.

Seminary professors charged with training missionaries may refuse to teach about Satan, too. They might skip over the Bible sections dealing with him, and never take the time to point out that the Apostle Paul was serious when he wrote Ephesians, Chapter 6. Consequently hundreds of missionaries begin each day confused and defeated. As a result, they ignore the primary work of the Lord, which is saving souls (Acts 26:18).

From this cause, new soldiers arrive at their "duty stations" unaware of the wiles of the devil. At the first hint of an enemy assault on their position, they shrink back and compromise. They may justify it by serving strictly in "humanitarian" endeavors instead. Why? Because they don't understand or believe that their opposition is spiritual. When this happens, Satan is given liberty to prowl about freely in their lives and the lives of those they are sent to deliver from the darkness of eternal death. They never get to the job they were sent to do.

Those who believe that God's Word is for today, and expect to see the enemy opposition, will do better than those who don't. It is by faith that we begin our march onto the battlefields each day. And Elizabeth Eliot said it best about the price we pay for stepping out in faith, *"Faith is not faith unless it contains an element of risk."* It may be risky, but there is nothing more rewarding than walking by faith rather than by sight. (2 Cor. 5:7).

The Army in Which I Choose to Fight

God's people have two armies. One set up for display with lovely guns, neat little soldiers-all-in-a-row, socially correct staffs schooled in etiquette—and distinguished generals swaggering through the ranks as if they were something in themselves. Its core is made of sunshine soldiers and fair-weather patriots who leave the dirty work to others. This army shows itself for a modest fee on any Sunday morning parade ground, one steeped in traditional salutes, precision drills, and weekend-warrior stamina. The other is a real army, composed entirely of enthusiastic soldier/saints in battle attire, who will not be put on display, but from whom impossible efforts are demanded. Their standard is the Word of God. The Sword of Truth is their primary weapon. This is the army in which I choose to fight. Occasionally I meet other soldiers who've made this choice. When I do, it's like an old soldier's dream, where the team is a team—everyone respecting the other's spiritual gifts and God-given authority, as if observing an unwritten law unto ourselves. And leading by humble experience, the generals, colonels, lieutenants and sergeants all follow the tough commandments of God's written Word. There is no compromise. This is the army in which I choose to fight.

Soldiering For God

In God's kingdom, obedience and discipline are mandatory. With these in place we are assured of a powerful walk and a fruitful prayer life for effective warfare.

After coming home from Vietnam I spent two years as a Drill Sergeant, training new troops preparing them for combat. Looking back on how I did certain things it is clear to me that some of the methods I emphasized to set standards were exactly what God expects of His soldiers as well.

Of all the things I drilled into these young men the most important were strict obedience to authority and learning rigid discipline…even under the most painful conditions. These two aspects of Army training were designed to save their lives, and the lives of their buddies in the months to come. They had to respond quickly to orders and they had to be disciplined team-players. This was essential for the survival of their units and each individual involved. Training for the daily battles that we are commissioned to fight in God's Army is no different.

In His Army we must adapt to new standards that may seem foreign to most of us. The Military Code of Conduct explicitly states "you will never surrender of your own free will." Well isn't that interesting that the very first thing we *have* to do to enlist into God's Army is *surrender* ourselves and our will to God! This has been tough for many veterans to do because we have been trained in the natural to never give up to the enemy. However, in God's ranks it is a prerequisite for the victory over darkness. Surrender is the very first thing we must do in order to be effective soldiers for Christ.

Remember: *"Submit therefore to God. (then) Resist the devil and he will flee from you"* (James 4:7.)

The Code of Conduct for a Soldier of Christ

Article I

I am one of God's fighting men. I walk by faith, not by sight. I conduct myself in a manner worthy of the Gospel of Christ. I will do nothing from empty conceit; but with humility of mind regard others as more important than myself. I serve the Lord, my God, and none other. I realize that no soldier in active service entangles himself in the affairs of daily civilian pursuits (i.e., man's politics, worldly concerns that are perishing). He does this in order that he may please only God, who enlisted him (2 Tim. 2:4).

Article II

I surrender of my own free will to the Lord, my God. If in command I will surrender my men to the Him, and strive to lead them in a way so that Jesus may take them all captive. After becoming a captive of Christ, I will never resist Him in any way. I will make no effort to escape. I will accept no favors from the enemy.

Article III

If I become a prisoner of war, I will make every effort to escape and aid others in escaping. I will resist Satan by submitting to Jesus Christ, my Lord and Savior. I will obey only the lawful orders of Jehovah God, and His canonized Scriptures. When questioned I will always be ready to give witness to the hope and glory of the Gospel of Christ to set the captives free.

Article IV

While fighting in God's army I will always remember that my fight is not against flesh and blood, but against the rulers and powers of the darkness of this world. I will condition myself to the proper utilization of the Word of God in all my battles. I will pray unceasingly as a means of warfare, and do all things without grumbling and complaining. I will strive to be a light to the world.

Article V

I will fit myself in the full armor of God every day . I will never attempt to do warfare without my armor being in place. (Ephesians 6)

After The Ambush

Article VI

I will let love be without hypocrisy, abhorring evil, clinging to good. I am devoted to others in brotherly love. I am diligent in praying for others, contributing to the needs of my fellow soldiers, and practicing hospitality. I choose to bless those who persecute me, and will not curse them. I rejoice with those who rejoice and weep with those who weep. I will never pay back evil for evil to anyone. I respect what is right in the sight of all men. I will never take my own revenge, and if my enemy is hungry, I will feed him; if he is thirsty I will give him something to drink. I will not allow myself to be overcome by evil.

Article VII

I will dispense true justice, and practice kindness and compassion for my brothers. I will never oppress the widow or orphan, the stranger or the poor, and I will never devise evil in my heart against another.

Article VIII

I will apply all diligence in my faith to supply moral excellence, knowledge, self-control, perseverance, godliness, brotherly kindness, and love to those around me, thereby ensuring that the entrance to the heavenly kingdom will be abundantly supplied to them all.

Article IX

I will love the Lord God with all my heart, soul and might. His words will always be on my heart. I will teach them to my sons and fellow soldiers. His words will always be bound in my heart and I will write them on my doorposts and gates.

Article X

I will never forget that I am one of God's fighting men, responsible for my actions, and dedicated to the principles, which make men free through the salvation of the Lord Jesus Christ. I will trust in my God forever.

...Amen.

Chapter Eight

Preparing For Battle

A LOT IS DONE PRIOR TO ANY COMBAT OPERATION. BEING PREPARED with good intelligence is mandatory. After all, nobody likes to get caught fumbling around in the dark...especially when lives are at stake. This is where reconnaissance comes into play.

Recon Teams

In Vietnam no operation, large or small, was ever conducted without a "recon" team going into the proposed battle area prior to deployment. The recon team's sole responsibility was to be the eyes and ears of the command. They surveyed the intended area of future battles, and then reported back with information needed to effectively launch and conduct a battle operation. The team was not too much unlike the spies that God ordered Moses to send to search out Canaan in Numbers 13:1-33. Listen to his orders instructing them how to conduct their "recon" mission. *"So Moses sent them to spy out the land of Canaan, and said to them, 'Go up this way into the South, and go up to the mountains, and see what the land is like: whether the people who dwell there are strong or weak, few or many; whether the land they dwell in is good or bad; whether the cities they inhabit are like camps or stronghold; whether the land is rich or poor; and whether there are forests there or not. Be of good courage. And bring some of the fruit of the land..."* (Num. 13:17-20). (With further study we see that this is one way God weeded out those soldiers who could be trusted or not with a mission. Only two came back with accurate reports.)

In Vietnam the LRRP (long-range reconnaissance patrols) teams had their own codes of operating. These men were hand-picked just like Moses carefully chose his men in the Book of Numbers. They were special men and went into the field with specific orders to observe and report. They were commanded *not* to make contact with the enemy unless it meant surviving to get back. When they went on each mission they kept in mind an acronym to keep them focused. S.A.L.U.T.E, Size, Activity, Location, Unit, Time, Equipment; those were the six elements of observation they were sent to report back with. Nothing else mattered. They were not sent to engage in combat, but were always prepared for it.

In conducting spiritual warfare in God's army our actions are not much different. It is part of our pre-planning strategies to know the enemy's size, activity, location, unit, time and equipment. If we disregard the signs along the trail and blindly walk into enemy territory we will surely not be as effective as God would want us to be. Reconning and discerning everything about the enemy is crucial in setting captives free.

Waiting for God

> *"...But those who wait on the Lord shall renew their strength; they shall mount up with wings like eagles, they shall run and not be weary, they shall walk and not faint"* Isaiah 40:31

After the recon reports come in, and are assessed, those who have the information received do not make a move until the chain of command has also assessed it. They do not step out or take any action until the high command constructs a strategy and gives the orders for them to move.

Here again, we do the same. We wait on the Lord. This is a powerful warfare technique and if we fail to utilize its wisdom, we will surely fail.

Waiting is so important in our battle planning and execution that it is worth looking at the word itself. In defining "wait" (Norman/French rt.) it means to "guard or watch". Our dictionaries define the word as: *"To stay in one place or remain in readiness or in anticipation—until something expected happens, or for someone to arrive or catch up."*

What the Scripture reveals to us is that waiting on God to always light up our path and plans demonstrates our obedience and willingness to fight His fight and not our own. If we do not receive orders…we do not make a move! It is pleasing to God for us to wait on Him…just as you would never get in front your point man on patrol, you must never get out in front of the Lord in the battle.

In the natural armed forces one of our duties was to stand (or walk) guard. It was a serious offense to leave your guard post before your watch was up. By not waiting to be relieved many consequences can happen:

1. Your fellow soldiers are left unprotected when they need your vigilance the most.
2. You inadvertently give aid to the enemy—you become an enemy yourself.
3. You lose the trust of those who depend on your commitment to watch *for* them.
4. The penalty could mean that you get court-martialed, and perhaps even a dishonorable discharge.

When you *wait* you are not doing it for yourself. You are first and foremost doing it in obedience to God. Secondly you are doing it as an act of protective love to those who depend on your sworn commitment to be a watchman when they are not looking.

Part of our commission is to use spiritual eyes to discern the ways of God (and His warnings). When we have His eyes we can effectively "walk point" for those who do not have these eyes. (*But the natural man cannot see the things of the Spirit of God: for they are foolishness to him; and he cannot know them, because they are spiritual in nature. 1 Corinthians 2*). If we fail to wait on God and step out to "do our own thing" we must rely on our own fleshly sight, and this what the enemy wants.

This is of utmost importance in pre-planning a combat operation.

The Ground

One crucial pre-planning topic is the nature of the terrain or ground you will be fighting on. You must have a clear understanding and knowledge of the terrain, or you are well advised not to attempt any tactical operations on it. It is the same in Christian ministry deployment. Know what ground, and whose ground, you are operating on before setting out. ("*...and see what the land is like: whether the people who dwell there are strong or weak, few or many; whether the land they dwell in is good or bad...*"

I simply look at the mission field as an area where a combat operation is being conducted. A Spirit-led soldier steps out and begins to minister God's truths to the unsaved. When he does this, it is like being dropped behind enemy lines—he enters Satan's territory, and nearly always smack-dab in the middle of his camp.

The mission field is not so much a physical country or territory as it is *spiritual terrain*...that makes this Satan's ground. Every time we go out to do the Lord's work we are on the enemy's turf. Most likely you will find this terrain right in the hearts of the men and women who live and work around you each day.

In summary; the mission field is not so much where you go, but what you do. Just like evangelism is not a formula, it is a life lived and given to others—no matter where you are.

A ministry field isn't necessarily a place like a jungle full of half-naked natives. It may not be a starving communist-ravaged third-world country either. This field is many places and many people. It is our neighborhoods, places of work, schools, social clubs, and even our churches. It may be your teenager's best friend that comes to visit. And, yes, it could be the bush people in a land far away. The mission field is people: people far and near, next door, or the uttermost parts of the earth. So, why is it that we tend to think that praying with naked heathens in a steaming jungle is the "work" of a missionary? Why do we not consider praying with the three-piece-suit heathens on Madison Avenue is not "missionary work"?

It's a mindset used against us to believe that missionaries are only those serving in steaming hot jungles. Mindsets are powerful, clandestine weapons of the devil. They are used against us to prevent widespread evangelism and discipleship. We need to know this to be combat-ready soldiers for God. A combat operation is the action you take in *your* mission field. The mission field God has led you to. Let it be done to the glory of the Lord!

Identifying the Enemy

Before an army goes to war it must know *whom* it is fighting. To know the enemy is to know its personality, its characteristics, its strengths, and its limitations. ("*...whether the people who dwell there are strong or weak, few or many...*"). Only a foolish commander would launch operations against a force not knowing its assets and liabilities. God gave Moses wisdom that we can pattern our warfare preparations after. (Num. 13)

After The Ambush

Almost immediately after getting saved in 1986 I was called into ministry. How did I know this? Well, I couldn't sit still until I had told as many veterans that I could about what He had done for me. I didn't have to go to missionary school and spend months and years planning a voyage to a foreign land; all I had to do was go find veterans and tell them what He would do for them if they would only surrender to His will.

In the beginning of this ministry to Vietnam veterans I thought the enemy I had to fight was stress, trauma, guilt, anger, drugs, alcohol, nightmares, and all the other symptoms and effects of Post-Traumatic Stress. Because I didn't know who the enemy was, the ministry was weak and ineffective. Those things that I thought were the enemy were only signs left along the trail by the real adversary—Satan.

As the weeks and months went by I could plainly see that if I just continued to fight against the "signs," I was going to lose the battle. I began to realize that I was not going to be able to snatch many of these vets from the clutches of their captor, and I knew something was missing.

Finally after much prayer, reading the Word, and good counsel from some mature brothers, (who knew something about spiritual warfare), I began to understand and get clarity on who the real enemy was, it was then that I began to walk in God's victory in ministering to others. God's ministry to veterans took on a whole new meaning for me. The ministry's effectiveness increased when I identified the correct enemy and applied that knowledge to my life and the lives of other veterans and their families.

As Christian soldiers we must be wise as serpents (and gentle a doves) in our warfare tactics—we have learned many things that God wants us to know about our enemy, it would be a shame to let it all remain hidden an unused. If we take a stand to use the lessons we learned we will be effective on the battlefield as we apply them.

Who is the Enemy?

Angels are the enemy. Fallen angels.

Satan (Lucifer) was the head archangel over the ranks of created beings in heaven long before God created Adam and Eve. He was thrown down because of his bragging, usurping spirit and his end has been declared in Isaiah 14.

When God ejected Satan and condemned him to the Lake of Fire at the end of time for his rebellious pride (Rev. 20:10), one third of the existing angels chose to rebel and go with Satan. These fallen angels are the demonic forces that harass and attack mankind. They are they referred to as stars along with all the other angels in Revelation 1:20 (*"As for the mystery of the seven stars which you saw in My right hand, and the seven golden lamp stands: the seven stars are the angels of the seven churches, and the seven lamp stands are the seven churches."*)

How do we know that Satan took one-third of the angels with him in his rebellion? In Revelation (12:3-4) we see it clearly: *"And another sign appeared in heaven: and behold, a great red dragon having seven heads and ten horns, and on his heads were seven diadems. And his tail swept away a third of the stars of heaven, and threw them to earth."*

Here are some facts about the enemy:

Let's begin with the leader, Satan. He is a real entity and foe.

Every New Testament writer teaches the existence of Satan and he is mentioned in seven of the Old Testament books. Jesus acknowledged and taught the existence of Satan in Matthew 13:39, and Luke 10:18, 11:18. Satan possesses intellect (1 Cor. 11:3), he has emotions (Rev. 12:17), he has a will (1 Tim. 2:26). Satan is a creature (Ezek. 28:14), he is a murderer (John 8:44), he is a liar (John 8:44), he is an accuser (Rev. 12:10), and he is the adversary (1 Peter 5:8). The practice and work of Satan is: He attempts to thwart the work of Christ (Matt. 2:16; John 8:44; Matt. 6:23). He deceives the nations (Rev. 20:3), he blinds the minds of unbelievers (2 Cor. 4:4), he snatches the word from the hearts of unbelievers (Luke 8:12). Satan tempts the Christian (Acts 5:3, 1 Cor. 7:5), he accuses and slanders them (12:10), he hinders the work of Christians (1 Thess. 2:18), he incites persecution against Christians (Rev. 2:10), and he deploys demonic forces against them in an attempt to defeat them (Eph. 6:11-12).

Next let's look at Satan's army—the demonic forces, or fallen angels who do Satan's bidding.

Demon forces...these are fallen angels. Satan is an angel, and is called prince of the demons (Matt. 12:24). Demons are the well-organized ranks of angels who follow Satan's orders to destroy mankind (Eph. 6:11-12). The characteristics of demons are: They are unclean spirits, and their doctrine leads to immorality (1 Tim. 4:1-2). They know Jesus (Mark 1:24) and their doom (Matt. 8:29), and the plan of salvation (James 2:19), and God can even use them to carrying out His purposes (1 Sam. 16:14; 2 Cor. 12:17).

The warfare tactics of demons are: They attempt to thwart the purpose of God (Dan. 10:10; Rev. 16:13-16). They inflict diseases (Matt. 9:33; Luke 13:11, 16). Demons can possess men (Matt. 4:24), they can possess animals (Mark 5:13). They oppose spiritual growth of God's children (Eph. 6:12), and they disseminate false propaganda, or doctrine (1 Tim. 4:1;).

So what are the primary Biblical defenses against Satan and his Army?

A. The believer should use his armor (Eph 6:11-18)

B. Christ intercedes for His followers (John 17:15)

C. The believer has authority to take a stand against Satan (James 4:7).

D. The believer has the authority to invoke the power o the Name of Jesus against any enemy attack and to bind and loose the enemy (Matt: 16:19, John 15:16, Mark 16:17).

E. Believers claim the blood of Jesus, pronounce their testimonies, and do not love their lives (even to death) as a priority. (Rev. 12:11).

As a word of encouragement, it is known that only *old* lions roar all the time. They are toothless and ineffective in the hunt, but they make a lot of noise, which scares all the other animals in the area. The killing is done mostly by the young lions who are relatively small and quieter. So in 1 Peter 5:8 (*"The devil prowls about like a roaring lion..."*) the devil is only *like* a roaring lion...he is not one. He is a faker and a toothless one at that. He lost his teeth at the Cross and wants us to believe that he is still something that we must be frightened of. When we are born again we have the authority to bind and loose, to heal and cast out devils...all in the name of Jesus! We need not worry (worry is sin) about the power of Satan, but be concerned about those whom he has deceived.

Chapter Nine

What is Spiritual Warfare?

*"Spiritual warfare is not just a prayer prayed or
a demon rebuked—it is a life lived."*
—Dean Sherman, YWAM

IT WOULD BE A MISTAKE TO ASSUME THAT EVERY CHRISTIAN KNOWS
what basic spiritual warfare is. To know about such things
depends on their "spiritual upbringing." Unfortunately many
church denominations look lightly, or not at all, on the war
waged by Satan on human beings. On the other hand, there
are some denominations or fellowships that become so en-
grossed in fighting the devil that strange ideas and offbeat
practices evolve.

So what is spiritual warfare in its base form?

Spiritual Warfare by definition is using the authority that
Christ gave His church to win victories over God's enemies.
As we see in this definition spiritual warfare isn't always just
praying to God; it is doing more. It is using the *authority* given
to us by Jesus to look demons right in the eye and render
them ineffective, *"In My name they will cast out demons"* (Mark
16:17b). We do not render evil powers ineffective on our own.
Always be mindful that it is God that does the deliverance...not

us! We use His authority as His children and heirs; but it is
His power—not ours.

By all means, we must pray for God to equip and em-
power us, but we also need to know that He will not necessarily bypass us to clobber the enemy forces. For an example,
there are only rare times in Scripture that we find God saying
that He will do the fighting for us. One is found in Malachi,
and interestingly enough, it has to do with our obedience in
the area of giving, *"Bring the whole tithe into the storehouse, so
that there may be food in My house, and test Me now in this,"*
says the Lord of hosts, *"if I will not open for you the windows of
heaven, and pour out for you a blessing until it overflows. Then I
will rebuke the devourer for you"* (Malachi 3:10-11a). (Perhaps
Christians who expect to be more victorious in warfare should
re-evaluate their views on giving portions of their substance
back to the Lord.)

Yes, the Commander expects us to engage the enemy
head-on, which isn't strictly praying. We authoritatively command demons to cease their activities and cast them away
(which is not prayer). It is all done by the power of the blood
of Jesus and the authority of His wonderful name. It is not a
complicated procedure—it is just speaking as Jesus would
speak…and on His behalf.

Warfare Strategies

The souls of men are the "property" of the strong man
(Satan) in Mark 3:27. Satan doesn't have any need for your
Mercedes Benz, home, gold, silver, or any other material possession, all he wants to do is take as many to hell with him
that he can. He works against the ministry we Christian soldiers do to snatch the lost from his hands. He tries to thwart
our preaching of the gospel at every opportunity, and wants
us to cease doing spiritual warfare. We are instructed in that
same Scripture (Mark 3:27) to move into action and take that
"property", so we know that it can be taken.

It is important to note here that we seldom, if ever, fight Satan face to face. In all the circumstances that we recognize as "demonic," or "satanic" Satan himself is not there directly causing it. He is not omnipresent; he cannot be everywhere there is demonic activity occurring. (That would be like thinking that we were fighting Ho Chi Minh face to face, when in reality we were engaged in combat with a little Viet Cong who represents Ho. In fact, Revelation 12:10b tells us where Satan spends most of his time, *"For the accuser of our brethren has been thrown down, who accuses them before our God day and night."* In other words, the devil spends every day and every night before the throne of God accusing us of our sins. How could he be in your bedroom causing a quarrel between you and your spouse when he is standing before God accusing you? He is not omnipresent (everywhere). It is vital to know that he has sent one of his demonic spirits to cause that quarrel, so address the demon ... not Satan!

I was at a Point Man veteran meeting one evening back in 1987. As we went around the table making introductions and hearing about how everyone's week had been going, we met one of the demons that Satan sends out to do his work. One of the veterans complained about an ongoing upheaval in his family. As he began to describe some of the impacting details of his family's problems his countenance began to change. Soon the complaining turned to a full blown demon attack. The vet rose to his feet and gripped the edge of the table in front of him. He began screaming and moaning at the top of his lungs, and we knew that he had to be delivered right then.

We began the assault on the enemy with warfare and prayer that went nonstop for almost two hours. Finally the breakthrough came when the Lord spoke a word of knowledge to one of the brothers. He told him that the Vietnamese demonic principality of Cau Dai was controlling this man. When we zeroed in and called Cau Dai onto the battlefield by name, he was identified and bound by the name and shed blood of Jesus. We were then able to cast it out of the veteran's life. The man was immediately released from years of agony, and began a brand new walk with Jesus that very hour even though he had been a professing Christian for over a decade.

The veteran was set free from a specific demon that had tormented he and his family for over thirteen years. His victory came because we listened to God and called out the demon by name just as Jesus did when he called the demon "Legion" to come out of the man in the Book of Mark. When we are doing spiritual warfare, we are fighting against Satan's agents (spirits or fallen angels) dispatched to harass and harm us. We are not fighting him directly! I believe it is fair to say that when we bind and loose, we must bind and loose "the spirit" involved. This gives us much more accuracy in our firepower against the "*. . . rulers, powers, world forces of this darkness, and spiritual forces of wickedness in the heavenly places*" (Ephesians 6:12).

It is important to note that you do not necessarily need to know the name of every demon you engage in combat. This is a false and deceptive notion from the enemy to weaken your strategy and distract you. In Vietnam, we certainly didn't have to know the name of every Viet Cong soldier before we could shoot at them; and they certainly didn't know our names. We just met on the battlefield and engaged each other in combat. No introductions were necessary—it's the same here. However, if the Lord does reveal the identity or name of a specific demon, your warfare will be much more effective if you call it by name (see Mark 5:9).

Warfare Principles

It is a simple, but rigorous, matter to fight in spiritual warfare—IF you follow the Word of God! There are several important Scriptures that need to be referred to for foundational purposes, and in these you will see the method that God has designed for believers to use in our daily battles against our avowed enemy, Satan.

First of all 1 John 3:8 states *"...The Son of God appeared for this purpose, that He might destroy the works of the devil."* It is clear that Jesus' mission of coming here in physical form was to do warfare and destroy the works of Satan. If *we* are now the manifested "Body" of Jesus Christ that *appears* in the world today then it only stands to reason that it is also our mission to do the same...destroy the works of the devil.

And how do we "destroy the works of the devil?" Let's look at Mark 3:27, where it states, *"But no one can enter the strong man's* (the devil) *house and plunder his property* (the souls of men) *unless he first binds the strong man, and then he will plunder his house* (which basically means to set the captives free).

So we need to destroy and hinder the work of the enemy by *binding* Satan. "I bind Satan (or any demon that I can call by name, i.e. the spirit of suicide, spirit of rage or anger, etc.) in the Name of Jesus!" But remember...we can do nothing by ourselves. (*"Truly, truly, I say to you, the Son can do nothing of Himself, unless it is something He sees the Father doing; for whatever the Father does these things the Son also does in like manner"* John 5:19-20:1.)

Along with doing nothing on our own comes the matter of knowing what protective armor the Lord has given us to **use** each day! Here again we emphasize Ephesians 6:10-18. This passage must be held onto and applied each day. We should make a conscious effort to put on the armor before beginning our daily activities. The sum total of the armor is Jesus (Romans 13:14). Put Him on and wear Him each day.

I have heard many teachers say that we Christians have no protection for our backsides when it comes to the armor God has provided. But I believe that a proper Commander would never leave his troops without a complete set of battle gear. Isaiah 58:8 tells us *"the glory of the Lord is our rear guard"*. This clearly states that we're covered, because that is what the Word says.

Our marching orders are stated in Acts 26:18; *"...to open their eyes so that they may turn from darkness to light and from the dominion of Satan to God, in order that they may receive forgiveness of sins and an inheritance among those who have been sanctified by faith in Me* (Jesus)." We must also understand the nature of our war. It isn't against flesh and blood but it is against spiritual oppression. (*"For though we walk in the flesh, we do not war according to the flesh, for the weapons of our warfare are not of the flesh, but divinely powerful for the destruction of fortresses"* 2 Corinthians 10:3.)

Chapter Ten

Weaponry

*"For though we walk in the flesh, we do not
war according to the flesh, for the weapons of our
warfare are not of the flesh, but divinely powerful
for the destruction of fortresses" (2 Corinthians
10:3-4).*

IN ORDER TO BE THE BEST WARRIORS FOR THE LORD, WE NEED TO know
the enemy's strengths as well our own, and it is important to
note that the weapons on both sides are not of a physical nature, but spiritual. As we check the Scripture this is very clear.

Looking at Revelation 12 we see this weaponry spelled
out. In verses 9 and 10 we see Satan's weapons are in the form
of two distinct activities: to deceive the world and to accuse
the brethren. Satan uses these powerful weapons to run his
prison camps and fight against us—the saints of God. However, the Lord has provided us (the saints) with three weapons to counter the two that Satan uses. Ours are described in
verse 11: We are to bank on the merits of the death of Christ,
". . . they overcame him because of the blood of the Lamb"; and
we are to be active in witnessing, *". . . the word of their testimony"*; and we are willing to make any sacrifice for the gospel, including our own death, *"and they did not love their life
even to death."*

After The Ambush

What wonderful, simple tools God has given us to fight the good fight with. We have the authority of His name, [1] *"Whatever you ask of the Father in My name, He may give to you"* (John 15:16). We have the continual cleansing power of His blood. We have the word of our testimony and (the one that gets Satan the most) we have the carefree hearts to know we are not afraid to sacrifice ourselves (even unto death) for our one and only Commander-in-chief...Jesus Christ. These are the most powerful weapons. There are no weapons in all creation that can stand against them.

The Full Armor

> *"Put on the full armor of God; that you may be able to stand firm against the schemes of the devil"*
> (Ephesians 6:11).

Putting on the armor is crucial in our daily walk (and battles) as Christians. Many Christians do not take the time, or make the effort to pray on the armor mentioned in Ephesians 6 before starting each day. This usually lays them wide open to unnecessary pitfalls that the enemy (Satan and his hordes) constructs against them throughout each day. Many of these traps along the trail are directly connected to

---

[1] It is important to note that using the *Name of Jesus* as a weapon is not just a mechanical parroting of words. Some believe they MUST invoke God's power by using the words "In the Name of Jesus" during prayer, or when ending their prayers. To think that our prayers will not be heard or answered if we don't end a prayer by saying "in the Name of Jesus" goes beyond legalism...it is borderline witchcraft. In John 15:16 Jesus is saying that as His servants and representatives we are authorized to use the *authority* of His name when we pray. Nothing else. To say we must end all prayers by saying the exact words "in the Name of Jesus" is taking the freedom of Christ and turning it into a form of bondage. As an example, if you call my office and a secretary answers the phone and she, or he, relays information from me to you, she is using the authority of my name. She is speaking for me in my absence, and I have given her the right to do so. To make my point; it would sound absurd for her to end the phone conversation by saying, "In the name of Chuck".

the curses, soul ties and other demonic activities we knowingly or unknowingly embraced while in S.E. Asia.

In Vietnam we never went on patrol without all our equipment and necessary items to survive combat. Through that experience we all became keenly aware of the importance of being prepared and protected before entering critical situations. Being in God's army is no different, and He expects us to take up His armor daily to repel the assaults of our enemy.

Being a good "Commander," God never sends His troops to the front lines without providing all the equipment they need. Ephesians 6:10 18 and Isaiah 58:8 is that equipment. I encourage you to study these scriptures (Ephesians 6:10-18, Isaiah 58:8) and memorize them. Make it a daily discipline to put on the full armor of God in prayer. Here is an example of how to do that:

"I put on the belt of truth, that today I speak and hear only the truth of God.

"I put on the breastplate of righteousness, that my heart is protected by God. That I would have a right standing before God and His throne today.

"I shod my feet with the gospel of peace, that everywhere I step God's peace will abound.

"I take up the shield of faith to ward off the fiery darts of the enemy Jesus, I proclaim You to be my shield; a shield that I can kneel down behind and seek protection from the enemy

"I put on the helmet of salvation, that my mind will be protected by God. Lord, transform my mind into the mind of Christ this day, that all thoughts that I have would be the thoughts of Jesus Himself.

"I take up the Sword of the Spirit, the Word of God, to wield against the enemy in time of warfare. I also pray that this Sword may be used to circumcise my own fleshly heart and to give me strength this day to rise above the sin that abounds always in my life and in this world.

"Lord, I thank You for protecting my backside with Your glory as proclaimed in Isaiah 58:8. The Lord God almighty is my rearguard, and I do not have to be afraid of what is behind me. I refuse evil and choose good just as Jesus did. Today, I refuse the will of Satan and choose the will of God!"

The Warfare is like Wrestling

In his spiritual warfare teaching series, Dean Sherman, *Youth With A Mission*, mentions a particular fact that is important to spiritual warriors. He calls it "wrestling." He takes the scripture passage of Ephesians 6:12, *"For we wrestle not against flesh and blood..."* and shows us further about the nature of our combat. We are in a wrestling match. In this type of match Satan is constantly sending his agents to wrestle with us. We cannot say, "Hold it, I'm tired. I need a rest." It is useless to say this because Satan's power will not back off. If you decide to take a little breather, the demonic enemy will continue to be all over you. They are relentless in their attack. However, one must never get the idea that Satan or his demons have power equal to, or outside, the realm of God's dominion. I have concluded that the devil and his demons cannot lay a hand on me unless the Lord lifts His protective hand from me first. He will surely do that if I am practicing sin and/or have unforgiveness in my heart. Or if there is a lesson of growth that God desires in my life (See Job 1:6-12) I may be in for a challenging exercise in faith.

Sherman then says, "Like the sport of wrestling, our warfare requires that we be consistent. We have to be alert in our mind (thoughts and imaginations), our heart (attitudes and emotions) and our mouth (spirit power) . ...A wrestler wins the wrestling match not only from superior strength, but with knowledge of the holds. (Here is wisdom). ...If you walk through life and know the wrestling holds, you can deal with things that come up . ...Walk constantly aware of Satan's schemes, that's knowing the holds!"

"'*We wrestle not against flesh and blood*' 'This statement,' Sherman goes on to say, 'is the key to the whole battle! The key is never battling flesh and blood. The Bible forbids battling flesh and blood. You never win by fighting a human being. God's kingdom has never been advanced through fighting people. It is advanced only through prayer! When faced with the temptation to fight people, we are to always pray first, resist the devil, assess honestly whether there is any truth in what a person is saying, and then humble ourselves. Don't battle in person (do it in prayer/warfare); continue to agree with God and His Word, keep strong in the faith, and maintain relationships at all costs.'"

In summarizing our warfare weapons, bear in mind: Satan attacks us primarily in two different ways. From Revelation 12:9-10 (1) he <u>deceives</u> the whole world and (2) he <u>accuses</u> them before our God day and night.

However, we overcome Satan primarily by *three* ways. From Revelation 12:11, (1) because of the <u>blood of the Lamb</u>. (2) because of the <u>word of our testimony</u>, and (3) <u>not loving our lives unto death</u>. It is not only interesting, but comforting as well, to see that God gave us one more weapon than Satan has to fight him with.

The bottom line is this: the battles have all been won! Our Order of Battle (the Bible) says that we win in the end. The end has already been decided...we need to walk in that. Be encouraged because the Word says, "*No weapon that is formed against you shall prosper; and every tongue that accuses you in judgment you will condemn. This is the heritage of the servants of the Lord, and their vindication is from Me, says the Lord*" (Isaiah 54:17).

Chapter Eleven

Fellowship with Enemy Forces

A SOLDIER NEVER FRATERNIZES WITH THE ENEMY. IT CAN BE A COURT-martial offense if he does. But a Christian's fellowship with Satan (and his hordes) without even knowing it, gives away our footholds on spiritual "ground."

Holding our ground is of utmost importance to soldiers in war. The ground we have gained by yielding and submitting to God's will is the very thing we need to continually fight for. However, we can lose great portions of our joy and victory (ground) by allowing the enemy access through our thoughts and actions. We can actually join forces with the enemy by our misconduct, better known as—sin!

Every time we sin without repenting (which means turning away and discontinuing to do it), we open a window of opportunity for the demons of hell to blow through our lives. The reason Jesus commanded the woman caught in adultery to *"go your way. From now on sin no more"* (John 8:11), was because He knew that her practice of sin was what was defeating her. Every time we practice our sin, we actively fellowship with enemy forces. This action alone gives the devil vital segments of "ground" that has been hard won through our fellowship and obedience to God. (It should be noted that John 1:8 states, *"If we say that we have no sin, we are deceiving ourselves, and the truth is not in us."*)

After The Ambush

There is a difference in "having" sin and "practicing" sin. Having sin refers to the sin nature, which we will have as long as we are on Earth. But practicing sin is the act of continuing to sin over and over with no true repentance. This "practicing" is what Jesus expects all of us to be rid of!

In the best-selling book, The Bait of Satan, John Bevere describes the kind of sin most of us practice without even realizing it. "One of his (Satan's) most deceptive and insidious kinds of bait is something every Christian has encountered. It is offense. Actually, offense itself is not deadly—if it stays in the trap. But if we pick it up and consume it and feed on it in our hearts, then we have become offended. Offended people produce much fruit, such as hurt, anger, outrage, jealousy, resentment, strife, bitterness, hatred and envy.

"Some of the consequences of picking up an offense are insults, attacks, wounding, division, separation, broken relationships, betrayal and backsliding. Often those who are offended do not even realize they are trapped. They are oblivious to their condition because they are so focused on the wrong that was done to them. They are in denial. The most effective way for the enemy to blind us is to cause us to focus on ourselves." Having "offense" is sin and needs to be dealt with.

The Weapon of Forgiveness

Many Vietnam veterans live with the sin of bitterness and unforgiveness, not realizing how destructive it is to them and others.

One summer I was a speaker at the yearly CBN (Christian Broadcasting Network) Vietnam Veteran Conference in Virginia. I was asked to give a workshop on anger management, but God had another plan. He wanted to touch every veteran in attendance in a special way in the area of bitterness and unforgiveness.

Not long after I started talking about anger, the mention of Jane Fonda's activity (most veterans consider it treason) against America during the Viet Vietnam War came up. The following is an account of what I wrote about that session not long after it happened:

"The room was suddenly silent. Every eye was fixed on me as I stood beside the speaker's lectern. An uneasy feeling gripped me, and a nasty little voice kept telling me I should not have said what I did.

"I had just spoken the unspeakable (the subject of forgiving Jane Fonda) before a group of over two hundred Vietnam veterans. I could see the many reactions on their faces. Some were shocked with unbelief and I could tell some wanted to take me outside, while others looked for reasons to leave the room. The Lord had led me to tell this room full of battle-worn warriors that I had forgiven Jane Fonda for her misdeeds during the 60's and 70's, and now I was encouraging them to do the same.

"After the initial jolt I shared with them how God had shown me what harboring my own unforgiveness for Fonda was doing to my life. He showed me that as long as I couldn't forgive her, I was in relational bondage to her. He spoke this to my heart, *As long as you cannot forgive Jane, you will have a spiritual relationship with her that doesn't please Me.* Hearing this it didn't take me long to repent and forgive her.

"I asked to see a show of hands of those who wanted to be free from this sin, and what this woman represented to them. Many hands shot into the air. Since most of them did not want to have a relationship with her, they were more than eager to do what they could to severe any ties. As I prayed for deliverance for these men, I heard the crash bars on the exit door bang open. Pausing I looked up just in time to see a big Marine in his wheelchair leave the room in a hurry. Later we learned that his name was Rob.

"Rob had been a hard-charging Marine in Vietnam until a machine-gun bullet caught him in the spine. He had been confined to a wheelchair for some twenty years, and had been saved only a couple of weeks at the time of the conference.

After The Ambush

When I saw him leave that day I didn't know what to think, but I was hoping he was not going for his gun.

"Thinking that Rob was disgusted with the idea of forgiving Jane Fonda, I sort of shrugged off his quick departure and commenced to pray for the men in the room. About an hour after the session we were all in the hallway getting drinking coffee and getting to know each other, when we received the surprise of our lives. Rob, who had not been out of his wheelchair for all those years, walked in the door and marched straight into the cheering arms of the dozens of veterans who had seen him leave the room during the session.

"I asked Rob what happened, and he said, 'I decided to give in and try praying to God that He would let me forgive Jane Fonda. When I said that prayer my legs suddenly began to tingle with feeling. I got so scared that I went straight to the VA hospital and they checked out my legs. Probing around they discovered I could feel things again. Then I just got up and walked out, leaving my wheelchair behind. Not only am I free from Jane Fonda, but I'm free from my wheelchair too.'

"This was a major victory in Rob's life and we all claimed a wonderful victory that day as well. I believe we were allowed a quick peek into the throne room of God while He performed an absolute miracle on this crippled Marine. He shows us that we can all be healed and set free from the ambushes of the devil if we only obey His Word. We can have the victory only when we lay our bitterness on His altar, and forgive those who have trespassed and offended us in the past."

Unforgiveness is sin. The most powerful spiritual warfare there is when the saints cease to practice sin. Close the window that you opened with your sin by truly repenting. When you do, the enemy has no access to your life.

Blind Spots...a Soldier's Demise

One of the most important aspects of identifying the enemy is not getting him confused with the work of God in our lives. I don't know how many times I have mistaken (and seen other Christians mistake) God's sovereign work in my life by blaming the circumstances on Satan. We must be careful to discern and pray for wisdom in our observations before going to war.

We humans are weak vessels, and prone to mistakes, however, the Lord *does* intend to equip us for the coming battles. He wants us to improve ourselves in His ways. What a tremendous relief to know that He is always faithful to be there with us and for us.

Every day Christian soldiers in ministries like Point Man have opportunities to see the schemes of the devil working against them and the veterans they work with. Where we greatly err is failing to see the ambushes and tripwires on the trail ahead of us in time. In a guerrilla war one cannot afford such laxness. Personally I've not always been able to recognize these sinister schemes when I should have and paid a heavy price for not maintaining combat readiness. Only by the grace and mercy of God do we continue to survive as we march, and there is great comfort in remembering that whatever the enemy intends for bad, God will turn to good—for those who hear and obey.

In all of this, it is important to mention that God is sovereign in bringing us along in the school called "life." He can use our weaknesses, or He can give Satan permission to sift us for the purpose of bringing us into alignment with His will (Job 1:12).

Not long ago, just after saying to myself (and in earshot of the devil), *Lord, I am in need of nothing,* 12 days later, to be exact, my life went upside down. Relationships went haywire, my business was gone and I was almost spiritually shipwrecked. Sometimes I wonder if I had said, *I am in need of nothing, except You, Lord,* would it have been different? The Lord knew my heart. He knew that I had drifted far from needing Him and He wanted to bring me back and He used just the right amount of personal "coercion" to make it happen. It was a hard lesson to go through, but it was even harder to finally admit that I had become a lazy Christian. I see more and more each day that because of His love for me He set in motion those circumstances to save me again and again. He brought me out of my comfort zone to *need* Him like I had when I first believed.

Throughout the ensuing months of heartache and grief I learned many things, but in one of the darkest moments of insecurity, stress, and guilt (the enemy had to throw in his bit of condemnation), the Lord showed up with a promise for me. He took me to Isaiah 30:20-22 and began to show me that for all my life blind-spots (shortcomings, "the plank", areas of fault, or willful ignorance of areas in my life that need improvement) had been used by Him to teach me lessons.

As I read the passages in Isaiah, ("...*And though the Lord gives you the bread of adversity and the water of affliction, yet your teachers will not be hidden any longer, but your eyes shall see your teachers. Your ears shall hear a word behind you, saying, 'This is the way, walk in it,' whenever you turn to the right hand , or whenever you turn to the left.*") I began to see how my blind spots had gotten me into many spiritual dark holes. God was telling me that He was going to bring me to another place in Him and increase my "sight." His promise that my blind spots (my "teachers") would now be obvious to me and I would see them clearly as situations presented themselves. Since that time the surprises and ambushes have been less, and I'm getting much better at discerning (and heading off) things that otherwise would have caused a conflict or problem.

I don't think this word is just for me alone. I believe it is a word for all believers. Be encouraged to read it and meditate on it. It is an important promise, and more equipping from the Lord in our continued warfare strategies.

The devil uses our blind spots in some very subtle ways, and many times it is difficult to see him lurking behind the dark shadows of bad situations, but believe me—he is there! We just need to pray for God to show us more of these blind spots, and then train ourselves to quickly recognize the devil in our circumstances. This way we don't give him any more ground than necessary.

As veterans, who are now civilians in the world, we maintain the march through life and the discovery process continues. One of the most interesting and perplexing blind spots resulting from our war experiences is the on-going subject of Post-Traumatic Stress Disorder. It is interesting to see that so many Vietnam veterans today are just now discovering that Vietnam messed them up in some way. Nearly every day I find something new about how my life has been affected, and shaped by PTSD since Vietnam.

As soldiers for the King we need to be alert for every possible way the enemy can take us out, ("*Be on guard; stand firm in the faith; be men of courage; be strong*" 1 Corinthians 16:13), and getting a promise from the Lord that our blind spots will be brought out into the open is an incredible leap forward in our warfare, our walk, our relationships with people, and most of all…our relationship with God.

Chapter Twelve

Anger...Unlocking the Door to Break the Curses

VA Studies - Anger in Vietnam Veterans - Department of Veterans Affairs Puget Sound Health Care System, Seattle, WA 98108, USA.

This study examined the effects of combat exposure and Post-Traumatic stress disorder (PTSD) on dimensions of anger in Vietnam veterans. Vietnam combat veterans were compared with Vietnam era veterans without war zone duty on the Multidimensional Anger Inventory (MAI).

Combat veterans were not significantly more angry than their veteran peers who did not serve in SoutheastAsia. Additionally, various parameters of war zone duty were not highly associated with anger scores. However, combat veterans with PTSD scored significantly higher than veterans without PTSD on measures of anger arousal, range of anger eliciting situations, hostile attitudinal outlook, and tendency to hold anger in. These results suggest that PTSD, rather than war zone duty, is associated with various dimensions of anger affect.

PMID: 10360617, UI: 99287362

————J Trauma Stress 1998 Oct;11(4):731-42

Boston Department of Veterans Affairs Medical Center, National Center for Posttraumatic Stress Disorder, USA.

After The Ambush

This study examined the association between symptoms of Post-Traumatic Stress Disorder (PTSD) in male Vietnam veterans and their use of aggressive behavior in relationships with intimate female partners. 50 couples participated in the study. Veterans reported on their PTSD symptoms, and veterans and partners completed measures assessing the veterans' use of physical, verbal and psychological aggression during the preceding year as well as measures of their own perceptions of problems in the relationship.

Results indicated that PTSD symptomology places veterans at increased risk for perpetrating relationship aggression against their partners. The association between veterans' PTSD symptoms and their use of aggression in relationships was mediated by relationship problems. Clinical implications of these findings and suggestions for future research are discussed.
PMID: 9125790, UI: 97270755
Interpersonal and self-reported hostility among combat veterans with and without Post-Traumatic stress disorder.
Duke University Medical Center, Department of Psychiatry, Durham, North Carolina 27705, USA.

The present study investigated self-reported and interpersonal hostility in 70 Vietnam combat veterans with and without Post-Traumatic stress disorder (PTSD) and 60 comparison community volunteer subjects. Veterans were 50 help seeking, male Vietnam combat veterans with PTSD and 20 non-help seeking male combat veterans without PTSD. Vietnam veterans with PTSD not only reported more hostility than non-PTSD veterans and healthy community volunteers, but also reacted behaviorally with more hostility during an interpersonal interaction. Compared to veterans without PTSD, veterans with PTSD reported significantly higher levels of hostility and demonstrated significantly greater nonverbal expressions of hostility during an interpersonal task.

These results suggest that the level of hostility in PTSD combat veterans may be high as compared to comparison groups. The implications of these results and possible research directions are presented. PMID: 8731551, UI: 96301518

Anger's Power to Hold Curses in Place

There are *keys* to the spiritual warfare strategies the Lord provides for us when meeting the daily assaults from the enemy. He gives us these keys through revelation, knowledge, and many of the other gifts to the Body of Christ. It is, therefore, the utmost importance to let the Holy Spirit interpret God's Word on how we are to take action in every situation. He interprets the Word for us and always points us in the direction of Jesus—Who is the Word.

Since the three (3) curses play such a significant part of setting Vietnam veterans free, there is one key that needs to be inserted and turned to unlock these curses. That key actually focuses on one of the curses—the curse of anger.

Like every building has a cornerstone for strength and stability, so every evil curse has a key element holding it in place. I believe that if the curse of anger (or spirit of) is dealt with the other two curses (no peace and wandering) will automatically be subdued as well.

The "spirit" of anger is different than just being angry; it is a power force that emits threats to those around us. Most of the time we do not even realize we are putting off these "vibes." Remember back in the '60's there was the song by the Beach Boys titled, *I'm Picking Up Good Vibrations*? Well, that is exactly what the "spirit of" means. It exudes from people on a spiritual level, and even though people around may not understand why they feel the way they do, they "pick up on it." As sensitive beings in two universes at once, we are affected by these "vibes" and react to it on a physical level as well.

When we have the "spirit of anger" people walk on eggshells around us—and even though we haven't done anything outwardly to give them reason to be afraid us, they are almost terrorized at the thought of upsetting us. We can have a smile on our faces and do kind things, but we still may be emitting a "feeling" that if someone screws up around us we will be the first to condemn or chastise them for their mistake. If this is happening to you, then you have the "spirit of anger," and you need to deal with it.

A classic Biblical example of people having a "spirit of," and not realizing they had it, was in Luke 9:51-56. *"It was about time for Jesus to be taken up into heaven. He turned toward Jerusalem and was sure that nothing would stop Him from going. He sent men on ahead of Him. They came to a town in Samaria. There they got things ready for Jesus. The people did not want Him there because they knew He was on His way to Jerusalem. James and John, His followers, saw this. They said, 'Lord, do You want us to speak so fire will come down from heaven and burn them as Elijah did?' Jesus turned and spoke sharp words to them, (He said, 'You do not know what kind of spirit you have. The Son of Man did not come to destroy men's lives. He came to save them from the punishment of sin.' They went on their way to another town."*

When Jesus said, *"You do not know what kind of spirit you have"*, He meant that they didn't have a clue what kind of vibrations their spirits were emitting. He did not like it when they got angry! Contrary to popular Christian belief, nowhere in the Bible does it mention that man can have anger. God can certainly have anger, but men cannot. If they do, it is sin!

There is NO Biblical justification for anger or the spirit of anger. In fact, how many times have you had someone say, "Well a little anger is okay, or I had "righteous indignation"?

Those words in the phrase, *righteous indignation*, are never used together in the Scriptures. The only adjectives used to describe "indignation" are "great" and "fiery." They are used four times in Scripture. Twice it is God's "great or fiery indignation" and twice it is man's "great indignation." The indignation of God is righteous wrath. The indignation of man is sin.

Psalm 37:8 says, *"cease from anger and forsake wrath."* (Notice that it does not say, "keep spiritual anger and forsake carnal anger.")

Anger...Unlocking the Door to Break the Curses

If God ever gave "righteous indignation" to man that man would make it unrighteous indignation immediately. Look at Samson. The moment he got angry, he stopped fighting for the Lord and started carrying out his own personal vengeance. He fought in his flesh when he got angry.

Anger in man is the works of the flesh, and nothing else. To be angry or to allow yourself to be controlled by a "spirit of anger" is a serious liability and it leads to death and destruction.

Ephesians 4:31 clearly states that God expects us to put away all anger from our lives ("...let ALL wrath and anger be put away from you."). We must do this to be his best soldier. I believe controlling our anger is the key, and necessary ingredient, to breaking permanently free from the curses put on Vietnam veterans by those Buddhist monks.

Accountability is the action to take. Praying for deliverance from anger is a good thing, but it will take the buddy system to beat it for good. Proverbs 19:19 states, *"A man of great wrath shall suffer punishment: for if you deliver him, you will have to do it again."* That's right...we can get delivered over and over again from anger but it won't be until we are willing to pay something that personally costs us each time we get angry, it is doubtful that we will stay delivered from it. Make a deal with your spouse, or a trusted friend, and agree to give up something of personal value every time they see you get angry, or even feel that you are emitting the anger "vibes." Pay the price and see the results. It will work if you really want to lick this thing.

Anger Disqualifies You

In a court of law the judge presiding is not allowed to get angry. If he or she does in the course of a trial, they will be disqualified from the case.

As Christians we stand in a courtroom every day. Our opponent stands before the Judge (Rev. 12:10) and accuses each one of us of our sins past and present. God is not angered by accusations against us. He has already passed judgment on him and his end has been spelled out—both Satan and God are well aware of this. It is pointless for God to be angered by our enemy's attempt at slander so He remains unmoved and faithful in His decisions about washing our sins away past, present...and future.

Any anger we display in this courtroom though, serves to work against *us*. Our anger leads to more sin and more accusation—it disqualifies us from any credibility we are establishing in the courtroom. So the next time you feel anger rising up, remember that no anger is justified. (No, not even "righteous indignation"). To let our anger get loose gives into the flesh, and this is what disqualifies us. Satan wants you to get angry. It is his way of disqualifying you from having relationships and destroying your testimony for the Lord.

Anger is sin and it leads to death (James 1:14-15). And it goes like this: We get tempted to let our anger out, then Satan comes in and entices us, we then conceive a way or plan on how to act it out, next we act on the plan, and then the separation (death) from God comes. It may only take seconds for this sequence to happen, but each time it will be just like that. When we sin and move away from the Spirit and into our flesh, we disqualify ourselves. We are disqualified to continue any dialogue, offer any advice, exert any authority, or even show any meaningful love. The only way to turn it around is to repent for the anger (this includes figuring out a way to keep it from repeating—which is maintaining the discipline of accountability). After the repentance we must walk in a continual state of forgiveness. Like David, the apple of God's eye, we must be quick to repent. It is the only way to stay qualified for active duty in God's army.

Chapter Thirteen

The Act of War...
Let's Fight!

Breaking Free From the Ambush

NOW THAT WE HAVE SHOWN THE LIGHT OF TRUTH ON SOME OF Satan's ambush tactics (which have been affecting veterans and their families for almost a quarter of a century) it is only appropriate to move into the battle to meet the enemy head-on. It is imperative that we do so strictly according to the Word of God.

*Note: It is also important to know that it we cannot break free from Satan's ambush and fight in this spiritual war unless we have been born-again according to John 3:3, "*Truly, truly, I say to you, unless one is born again, he cannot see the kingdom of God.*" If you have read this far in this book and haven't said the prayer of Salvation, don't continue on until you do. It is only the committed believer who has the power from the Lord to fight in this war. (Acts 19:14-19). Believe in your heart and pray.

A Model Prayer for Salvation

"Father God, I come to you in the name of Jesus. I ask you to forgive me for all my past sins, including my rejection of Jesus Christ as Lord and Savior. I confess that Jesus is my

After The Ambush

Lord, and believe in my heart that He died for my sins and You raised Him from the dead on the third day. I now receive your forgiveness and Your life into my spirit. I am now Your soldier, enlisted to serve You as the One True God. Thank You Father for saving my soul through Your Son, Jesus Christ my Lord. Amen"

> *"And you shall know the truth, and the truth shall make you free"* John 8:31.

Total freedom is the promise to us through Jesus Christ our Lord. If we are to have it we must address and, attend to, some problems resident from the past. Veteran believers will be disabled until they gain the victory in the areas presented in this section.

Satan is a legalist. He knows his rights and will always take them. For instance, he will use unforgiveness as grounds to torment and refusal to leave. When he has such legal rights, no amount of ministry will bring relief until those rights are removed. So, if you have unforgiveness it is imperative that you deal with it before you begin to enter warfare.

Unforgiveness

> *"And his lord moved with anger, handed him over to the torturers until he should repay all that was owed him. So shall My heavenly Father also do to you, if each of you does not forgive his brother from your heart"* Matthew 18:34-35.

We *must* forgive. Unforgiveness is the root cause of most infirmities and personal problems. The Scriptures insist that we forgive if we are to be forgiven and have our prayers answered. The damaging effect of unforgiveness is the gall of bitterness deposited into our innermost being. Most infirmities are the result of the leavening of bitterness working its effects on our bodies.

God revealed the relationship between bitterness and infirmities at the waters of Marah (Exodus 15). As He sweetened the bitter waters He revealed a new attribute of His Nature: (*I am the Lord that healeth thee.*)

A bitter experience calls for a God who brings physical healing. True forgiveness cannot be initiated by emotions or feelings. It is set in motion by an intellectual decision. We must never "feel like" forgiving...we must exercise our will and decide to forgive.

Forgiveness model prayer:

Father, in the Name of Jesus, I have a confession to make; I have not loved, but have resented certain people and groups who have hurt or disappointed me. I have held unforgiveness in my heart. I call upon you now, Father, to help me forgive them. In the Name of Jesus, I now forgive: (Name every living or dead person, group, institution or organization that the Holy Spirit brings to mind. Forgive ALL hurts, disappointments and pain caused by any of these.) Father, in the Name of Jesus, I now forgive myself.

Note: It is most effective to speak audibly when repeating these prayers. Give the Holy Spirit plenty of time to show everything necessary. Sometimes you'll be prompted to deal with situations you had considered settled. It may require weeks or months of repeated prayer before the emotional feelings of resentment are completely gone. It is not necessary to forget. But you must forgive until you hurt no more.

Curses

"Christ redeemed us from the curse of the law,
having become a curse for us—for it is written,
cursed is every one that hangs on a tree"
Galatians 3:13.

After The Ambush

Contrary to popular opinion, curses are absolutely real. All one has to do is look at the three curses that are said to have been cast on Vietnam veterans...(1) wandering men (2) angry men (3) never find peace...to see the fruit. These three curses are an exact duplicate of many-troubled veteran's lives today. Curses are causing havoc in many lives now...even the lives of Believers!

Jesus approached a fig tree one day. Finding no fruit on it, He said to the tree, *"May no one ever eat fruit from you again.' 'The next morning as He and the disciples went along, they saw the fig tree withered from its roots. Peter said: 'Rabbi, look! The fig tree you cursed has withered!'* (Mark 11).

By speaking against the fig tree, Jesus brought a curse upon it. A curse is defined as: "uttering a wish of evil against one; to imprecate evil; to call for mischief or injury to fall upon; to execrate, to bring evil upon or to; blast, vex, harass or torment with great calamities.

Curses are activated through spoken words. The Scriptures tell us that words are not mere sounds on the lips, but life and death are in the power of the tongue. Words are agents sent forth for good or bad for us or for others.

Read about the blessings and curses in Deuteronomy 27 through 30. When Moses spoke these words to the people, blessings and curses were activated for all time. Jesus came to redeem us from these curses brought on by our sin. But to protect ourselves from curses we must walk in obedience to the principles in God's Word.

Sin opens the door for curses to come into our lives. Sometimes when ministering to others, we reach an impasse. We come to a standstill, and seemingly dead end. Rebuking the demons, praying, confessing the Word, even fasting won't break the enemy's hold. It is time to begin to seek revelation through the Holy Spirit to show us what curse it is that needs to be broken, and what sin is holding it in place. (Especially look for who is angry or has the spirit of anger).

After breaking the curse verbally, the deliverance follows. When folks can't get free, there is ALWAYS a reason. Sometimes it's because of curses that haven't been broken through the power of the blood and the spoken word. (*"They overcame him* (Satan) *by the blood of the Lamb AND by the word of their testimony"*), but it is wise to always look for unconfessed, unrepented sins before moving forward.

Curses act as shields and fences around demon spirits. These evil spirits can be invoked to manifest during ministry, but they will not and cannot come out until the curse or curses have been discerned and broken.

Breaking The Curses

Note: To break curses, refer to Galatians 3:13 and Colossians 2:14. Read these verses aloud. Also use the following prayer:

Model prayer for breaking curses:
(Read aloud)

Heavenly Father, in the Name of Jesus, I am truly your child. I have been purchased by the blood of your Son Jesus Christ and I belong to you. I do not belong to the Devil. The Devil has no right to me and no power over me because of the precious blood of Jesus. Father, you have known my sins. I confess them all. I repent of them all now. I ask you to forgive me. Forgive me of every sin and remove the stains from my heart and my life...for your Word tells me that when I confess my sin, you will forgive me of my sin and will cleanse me of all unrighteousness. I not only confess my own sin, but I confess the sins that were committed by my parents, grandparents and great-grandparents—sins that introduced curses into my family. I confess those sins to you that the power of the curse might be broken through the shed blood of the Lord Jesus Christ.

After The Ambush

In the Name of Jesus, I now rebuke the wicked spirits involved and break loose myself and my family from my own sins, the sins of my ancestors or from any other person. I am redeemed from the curse of the law. I break the power of every spoken curse...of every evil that came out of my mouth. I take back all ground I ever yielded to the Devil and establish myself in faith in the Lord Jesus and claim the blessing rather than the curse. I break the power of every evil word that was knowingly or unknown unknowingly spoken against me by any other person, or cult. I cancel that spoken word and the power of the curse in the authority of the Name of Jesus Christ.

I believe in your power, Lord Jesus. I believe in our redemption. I believe in my heart you are my Deliverer. I confess you with my mouth and I confess that the power of every curse is now broken in the authority of your Name. I command every evil spirit that has come in through the door of that curse to leave me NOW, in the Name of Jesus Christ.

Soul Ties

> *"Now it came about when he had finished speaking to Saul, that the soul of Jonathan was knit to the soul of David, and Jonathan loved him as himself"* 1 Samuel 18:1.

Soul ties are spiritual knittings formed through intense relationships such as with spouses and close friends. Some soul ties are not good. In the Spirit, soul ties resemble an umbilical cord reaching from one person to another. Until this cord is severed, it is impossible to break loose from an undesirable relationship.

It is possible to have soul ties with a group or organization, and most ungodly organizations find their power over people through this spiritual action. Herein lies the manipulative power of cults. Prayer and spiritual warfare should break all knittings of demonic nature. Of particular concern are relationships with ex-spouses, sexual partners (prostitutes, etc.), dominating or controlling individuals and control groups or cults.

Ask the Heavenly Father to reveal any person or group causing bondages in your life. Break the soul ties one-by-one after you repeat the following prayer.

Model prayer for breaking soul ties:
(Read aloud)

In the Name of Jesus Christ of Nazareth I choose to put off all remaining soul ties with persons in the past that would bind or hinder my Christian growth and walk. I come against any such soul ties now. I reject them and put them off in the Name of the Lord Jesus Christ. Jesus Christ is my Victor and victory, my Sanctifier, sanctifying me unto the Body of Christ into liberty, unto freedom. Praise the Name of Jesus.

I declare every soul tie to be broken. I renounce each one in the Name of the Lord Jesus Christ. I declare any such bondage to be done with because I am cleansed by the shed blood of Jesus and born-again. His resurrection victory over the grave gives me power and authority over all such things.

Satan, I declare myself to be loosed from you and your demons. I declare myself to be bound only unto the liberated Body of Christ: to be knit together in love in the glorious liberty of the Children of God. I break the souls ties I have had with the following: (now name specifically any person, group, organization or thing that comes to mind).

In the Name of the Lord Jesus Christ of Nazareth, I declare myself free from the cords, restraints, and tentacles of soul ties and command all personality spirits of any other person or persons to leave me NOW! Thank you Jesus. AMEN!

Chapter Fourteen

Truth—A Most Powerful Weapon in Your Arsenal

"Truth not experienced is no better than absolute error." A. W Tozer

As with many vital tools the Lord has used to instruct His warriors over the centuries, many come in the form of nuggets of gold from little known places and people. The following excerpt surfaces from an existence of relative obscurity. I have included it here because it highlights and sums up much of what we have talked about in this book. It is a real-life example of what this war is all about. It is very beneficial in helping us address the various aspects of our war. It is part of the lessons learned in an unseen war.

A few years ago a missionary friend visited our headquarters in Point Man Ministries and passed along "Chapter VI" of a book that was never completed or published. He picked it up on one of his many journeys for the Lord. "Chapter VI" is one of those rare works that crosses denominational barriers in teaching on a topic that has been shrouded with controversy. Mr. Wilbur Pickering speaks with knowledge akin to Josh McDowell and the common sense of Dean Sherman in regards to spiritual warfare. Pickering's accounts are from first-hand experience on the mission field, and there is little doubt that this writing has God's fingerprints on it.

"Chapter VI" will stretch your Christian walk. After reading it you will be convinced, like I was, that it was written by a battle-tested man who obviously was commissioned by God to share it with us. Wilbur Pickering was a missionary to Brazil, and after failing on his first missionary assignment, he came home to begin a search for truth in the area of spiritual warfare. What he writes here is vital information that every Christian warrior should have to prepare for the work of the Great Commission. We in Point Man have found it to be a powerful weapon in the hands of Christian soldiers. Here it is:

"Chapter VI"— A Missionary's Story

"Now let's consider the words of the Lord Jesus that we find in Acts 26:18. Paul is recounting, years afterward, the encounter he had with Him on the road to Damascus. Here's his story: *'13 At midday, O king, along the road I saw a light from heaven, brighter than the sun, shining around me and those who journeyed with me. 14 And when we all had fallen to the ground, I heard a voice speaking to me and saying in the Hebrew language, 'Saul, Saul, why are you persecuting me? It is hard for you to kick against the goads.' 15 So I said, 'Who are you, Lord?' And he said, I am Jesus, whom you are persecuting. 16 But rise and stand on your feet; for I have appeared to you for this purpose, to make you a minister and a witness both of the things which you have seen and of the things which I will yet reveal to you. 17 1 will deliver you from the people, as well as from the Gentiles to whom I now send you, 18 to open their eyes and to bring them back, from darkness to light and from the power of Satan to God, so that they may receive forgiveness of sins and an inheritance among those who are sanctified by faith in me.*

"Of specific interest to us here is the missionary commission that Paul (he was called Saul then) received...Matthew 28:19, Mark 16:15 and Acts 1:8 took place between the resurrection and the ascension, but to commission Paul, Jesus returned from Heaven! One other detail deserves special notice-the responsibility that Paul received was primarily for the nations, ("Gentiles" is a translation of the same word that in Mt. 28:19 is rendered "nations"). For these reasons it seems that this missionary commission takes on a special importance for us. And all the more so for whoever is going to do transcultural work. So let's consider this commission in more detail.

Paul's Missionary Commission

"Paul is sent to the nations, (defined ethnically) '...to open their eyes and bring them back, from darkness to light and from the power of Satan to God, so that they may receive forgiveness of sins and a place among those who are sanctified by faith in Me.' In other words, before someone can receive forgiveness of sins, even that someone must be freed from the power of Satan! Were you aware of that? Well, there it is. Before a person can be saved, someone must do something about Satan's influence upon him.

"The Lord Jesus had already said the same thing in different words during His earthly ministry. We find it in Mark 3:27. 'No man can plunder the strong man's goods, invading his house, unless he first bind the strong man; then he may plunder his house.' I have used the definite article with the first occurrence of 'strongman' because the Greek text has it, the point being that this particular strong man has already been introduced in the immediate context. 'The strongman' here is Satan. (The Jewish leaders tried to explain Jesus' authority over the demons by saying that He expelled them by the power of Beelzebub, prince of the demons. In His retort Jesus doesn't waste time with that name but uses the enemy's proper name, Satan.)

"So then, the Lord Jesus declares that it is impossible to steal Satan's goods unless you bind him first. And what might be the nature of those 'goods' be? In the context (of the above Scripture) Jesus had (just) delivered someone from a demon that caused blindness and dumbness. In their comments the scribes and Pharisees include other instances where Jesus had expelled demons. It seems clear that the 'goods' are people who are subject to Satan's power, in one way or another. Thus we have the same essential truth as that declared in Acts 26:18—we have to do something about Satan's power over a person so that he or she can be saved! But what does Satan do to people that would make it necessary to 'bind' him?

"We find the answer in 2 Corinthians 4:4. Let's begin with verse 3. *'If our gospel is veiled it is veiled to them who are perishing, in whom the god of this age has blinded the minds of the unbelievers so that the light of the gospel of the glory of Christ, who is the image of God, should not shine in them.'* The Text clearly states that Satan, 'the god of this world,' is in the business of blinding the minds of unbelievers when they hear the Gospel, so they won't understand, so they won't be convicted, so they won't repent and convert.

"This is a terrible truth, the most terrible truth in the world, at least as I see it. The enemy has access to our minds, access in the sense that he has the power/ability to invade them, whether by introducing thoughts or by jamming our reasoning. The Lord Jesus had already declared this truth previously, when He explained the parable of the sower. *'These are the ones by the wayside where the word is sown; but, as soon as they hear it Satan comes and takes away the word that was planted in their hearts'* (Mk. 4:15). In the parallel passage in Luke 8:12 Jesus adds the following words: *'lest they believe and be saved.'* Note that the Word is already in the mind or heart of the person, but then Satan comes, invades the mind and 'takes away' that Word. I'm not sure just how this intrusion by the enemy works, perhaps he causes a mental block of some sort, but the practical effect is that the Word becomes ineffective, as if the person hadn't even heard it.

Truth ... A Most Powerful Weapon in Your Arsenal

The Strategic Effect

"It seems obvious to me that whoever doesn't take this truth into account will be condemning himself to produce little effect in the spiritual realm, to work hard and achieve little. And isn't that exactly what we see? We preach, we evangelize, we speak and do so much, and yet the results are usually sparse, especially the lasting ones. So much so that we easily become discouraged and think of quitting. Isn't that so? But my brother, before preaching or talking did you give yourself the trouble to forbid the enemy's interference in the thoughts of your hearer? If not, what do you expect? It was Jesus Himself, God the Son here in this world, who made it clear that we must bind Satan in order to be able to remove people from his 'house.' We must bind Satan so as to avoid his interference in the minds of those who are being evangelized. (I will explain how to bind Satan later when I discuss the weapons that are at our disposal.) Now then, this 'coin' has two sides: our efficiency and our success depend upon our binding the enemy; but if we don't bind him we become his accomplices, because by permitting his interference without doing anything about it we cooperate with him! Can you imagine that? Actually, I suspect that few have in fact 'imagined' since these truths receive little or no mention in our churches, institutes and seminaries, at least so far. But really, brethren, the time has come, don't you think?

"I went to the Amazon jungle in 1963 in order to begin our ministry among the Apuring people (along the Purus river in the state of Amazonas, Brazil). So far as I know I was the first one to challenge Satan's dominion over this people, a total domination down through the centuries. My basic purpose in being there was to see if I could remove that people from Satan's house and take them to Jesus' house, if I could transfer them from the kingdom of darkness to the kingdom of light. But unfortunately, in spite of a Master of Theology degree and having read the Bible through several times, I was not aware of these truths. I got clobbered!

After The Ambush

"I got it without mercy, until I had had enough. Satan wiped the floor with me. He didn't think my idea was the least bit funny, and I didn't know how to defend myself. Actually, I didn't really understand what was happening. You see I was skeptical about the activity of the demons. Oh yes, I knew that Satan and the demons exist, because the Bible is clear and emphatic on that score, but I knew very little about how they operate and virtually nothing about the use of our weapons, whether for defense or offense. My theological background, both formal and informal, was strictly 'traditional'— casting out demons and things of that sort was 'Pentecostal.' My professors transmitted the idea that a servant of Christ was untouchable or exempt from demonic attack; that sort of thing wouldn't be a problem for us.

"Anyhow, I got clobbered. First, my wife and I were attacked in the mind, (and then) in the body. Second, being skeptical on the subject I wasn't able to hide my skepticism. (These) people have to deal with demons. This relationship is central to their culture. Since they know that the demons both exist and attack them in various ways, as in fact they do indeed exist and attack, my skepticism disqualified me. I was there proposing to teach them about spiritual truth, about supernatural things, but was obviously ignorant about the central reality of their existence. I lost my credibility. Third, in consequence (of my skepticism and ignorance) I was unable to help or liberate them. I was unable to give them proof of Christ's power, and therefore of the value of the Gospel...Fourth, when you finally control the language and culture to the point where you can explain about Jesus-what He's like, what He did, what He taught—then, sooner or later, you will say that He expelled demons and cured the effects of their activity. At last you said something that the people really want to know. (As I've already explained, they 'worship' the demons out of necessity, not because they enjoy it, because they don't know of any benevolent power great enough to free them.) Now you have their attention and can expect this query: *Jesus has power over the demons?*

"At this point you have a choice: are you going to say that Jesus has power, or that He had it? What are you going to affirm? I imagine that you would say, 'Yes, He has!' Right? Only at that point a demon will challenge you to your face, attacking someone in the village. So now what do you do? You don't know how to cast out demons, you are skeptical about such things, and yet you affirm that Jesus has power over them. If you don't know how to impose the victory and power of Christ in that hour, if you can't prove that Jesus is greater, then you were just beating your gums. You will be demoralized. You lied! Worse yet, Jesus is demoralized too! Of course you are His only spokesman in that place and if you can't demonstrate His power, the people will certainly conclude that He doesn't have such power. Any doubt about that? Well, I got clobbered. I weep when I think on the little that I achieved among the Apuring people, on behalf of Christ's kingdom, compared with what I could and should have achieved, had I understood this missionary strategy of Christ: free the peoples from the power of Satan.

"And that's not all. The great majority of the missionaries actually working (and that have already worked) among the animistic peoples of the world are skeptical about these things, like I was. Sadly, our missionary organizations have not concerned themselves about this matter, as a rule. The missionaries are out there suffering, as I did, producing much less effect than they could produce. What a tragedy! What a waste, in every sense of the term! The strategic importance of this matter is tremendous. If one day we reach the point of sending out workers who are adequately prepared in this area and of having churches full of people who know how to conduct spiritual warfare, then we will finish reaching the world. (Even the Islamic world, which I believe to be the most difficult challenge that we face, should be reachable in this way, because they too are troubled by demons.)

"We have yet to comment upon the last phrase of Paul's commission, 'a place among those who are sanctified.' I would say that the primary reference of this phrase is to final sanctification, our position in Christ. It happens, however, that it could easily refer to our experience as well because what Satan and the demons do has a definite influence on our spiritual life and on the effectiveness of our ministry, as well as on our life in general.

"My, how the enemy messes up our lives, spoils our homes, dilutes our efficiency in the work! If we would convince ourselves about the extent of their activity and learn how to handle the spiritual weapons that Christ gives us we could simply transform our lives, our homes and our ministries. The majority of the people that God calls to transcultural mission will be defeated by Satan right here, they never get to the field. Of the few, relatively speaking, that do get to the mission field, half are removed from the running within four years—they return defeated to their home countries, and never again return to the mission field. Such have been the statistics of modern missions, but I sincerely believe that we can improve the picture dramatically. All we have to do is get serious about this missionary strategy of Christ: liberate people from the power of Satan. It is absolutely necessary that we recognize that we are at war.

The Spiritual War

"We are in a war whose sphere is universal and which provides the context from which everything we do derives its deepest importance. In Luke 11:23 the Lord Jesus said: *'Whoever is not for me is against me; and whoever does not gather with me scatters.'* Jesus does not allow neutrality you are either for or against, one or the other. Either we are gathering or else we are scattering and therefore there is no neutral ground. We may grant that a given object is presumably neutral in itself, but the use that we make of it will not be neutral. At the deepest level we either do things with a view to God's kingdom and glory! I or we do them for some other reason, and be that reason I what it may it will serve the interests of the enemy. *'Whoever does not gather with me, scatters.'* It follows that everything we do is invested with importance. Even the ordinary things that we usually do without thinking have consequences in the spiritual realm. We are at war, whether we know it or not and whether we like it or not.

"We can state the problem more precisely. Not only are we at war; we are on the front line. That is to say, there is lead flying around on all sides. To walk around on a field of battle without taking due precaution is simply stupid, too stupid; it is to guarantee that you will be hit. The more so when we are precisely the ones who are in the enemy's sights because we belong to Jesus.

"One of the principle passages on the spiritual war is Ephesians 6:10-19 (the full armor of God). It says plainly that our fight is not against people 'the wiles of the devil'; it speaks of 'the fiery darts of the wicked one.' It is urgent I that we know the enemy, but first I want to mention another factor.

The Guarantee of the Strategy

"In Hebrews 2:14 we find the truth that renders this strategy viable. '*Since, then, the children partake of of flesh and blood, he also himself likewise shared in the same things so that through his death he might destroy the one who had the power of death, that is, the devil.*' Why did Jesus die? To destroy Satan! Did you know that? Well it's true, and He succeeded! Hallelujah! Colossians 2:15, Ephesians 1:20 and John 16:11 speak of the defeat suffered by Satan and his angels, the demons. That's why we read that he 'had' the power of death (Hebrews was written after Christ's victory). In Revelation 1:18 the glorified Jesus declares: 'I have the keys of death and Hades.' Jesus won! It is Christ's victory that guarantees this strategy and makes it viable. We can, yes we can, liberate people from the power of Satan!

How Do Satan and the Demons Operate?

"Let's go directly to the Sacred Text. We'll begin with Luke 9:18-22:18 *'It came to pass that as he was alone praying his disciples came to him, and he asked them, saying, 'Who do the multitudes say that I am?' 19 'Answering they said, John the Baptist; others say, Elijah; still others say that one of the ancient prophets has resurrected.' 20 'He said to them, 'But you, who do you say that I am?' Peter answered and said, 'The Christ of God.' 21 Warning them he ordered them not to tell anyone, saying, 22 'It is necessary that the Son of man should suffer many things, that he be rejected by the elders, the chief priests and the scribes, that he be killed and that he rise from the dead on the third day.'*

"I wish to call attention to the grammatical Structure of this passage. Note the present participles: 'answering,' 'warning' and 'saying.' The effect of this structure is to signal continuous action. Verses 18-22 contain a single conversation. Having registered this fact let's move to the parallel passage in Matthew 16:13-23 that gives us more detail. Rather than transcribe the whole thing I will just comment on the added details. In verse 16 Peter answers, 'You are the Christ, Son of the Living God,' to which He responds, 'You are blessed, Simon, son of Jonah, because it was not of flesh and blood that revealed this to you but my Father who is in Heaven' (vs. 17). Skipping to verse 21 we have Jesus' declaration that He must suffer and die. 'With that Peter began to rebuke Him:' 'Far be it from you, Lord; this shall never happen to you!' (vs. 22). To which initiative Jesus answered, 'Get behind me, Satan!' (vs. 23).

"Well, that scares me; that sends shivers up my spine. Within three minutes, or five at the most (we saw in Luke that this was a single conversation), Peter spoke two times. The first time it was God who put the words in Peter's mouth. It was Jesus Christ, God the Son on earth, who explained the true nature of the transaction. Peter did not speak on his own but moved by the Father. So far so good. That God can do something like that comes as no surprise. It is the second time that is bothersome because this time it was Satan who put the words in Peter's mouth! Again, it is Jesus Christ, God the Son on earth, who explains the true nature of the transaction. When He uses the enemy's proper name, Satan, His meaning is inescapable. It really was Satan. The rules of language do not permit the "spiritualizing" of someone's proper name (unless it be in a secret code, which deliberately violates those rules—but that is not the case here). 'Gerald' always refers to someone of that name, and so with 'Samuel,' or 'Charles,' etc. 'Satan' here refers precisely to Satan. Once again we are face to face with the most terrible truth that there is in this life, at least as I see it. The enemy has access to our minds; he can put words in our mouths. I wish in the worst way that it wasn't true, but my wishes don't change reality.

They Attack Our Minds

"When I finally awakened to this truth I began to understand several things that used to happen to me. More than once I would be talking with someone, a serious conversation about the things of God, when all of a sudden words would come from my mouth that were simply unacceptable, words that destroyed the situation. As soon as I had spoken I knew it was bad, but it was too late; the other person would turn his back and leave. I was left dismayed and perplexed. How could I say something like that? Note well, it wasn't something I had been thinking about, that had been in my mind; no, I became aware of it only after I had spoken. For years I never found an answer, I couldn't figure out what happened to me, but now I know Some demon put those words in my mouth, and since I didn't realize such a thing was possible I fell into the trap. Now that no longer happens to me. Now I know how to defend myself.

"I know. You don't like this idea (neither do I); you don't want to accept it. Let's go slowly. Maybe you yourself never experienced anything like I just described but perhaps you have observed the following. It is routine, you can virtually count on it; in any meeting where the progress of the work is being handled (be it of the deacons, elders or trustees; of the board of a mission or a school; of a presbytery, synod or conference; in short, be it a small or large gathering) you can observe the following. Everything is going well, the blessed communion of the saints seems to be functioning, when all of a sudden someone says something he shouldn't, gratuitously, to hardly any good purpose. The climate of the meeting is ruined; you may as well go home for all the constructive progress that will now be made. Haven't you ever seen that happen? I bet you have; it is routine. You can even call that person aside, after the meeting, and ask: 'Tell me, please, why did you ever say that?' And if he is sincere, as he often is, he may answer something like this: 'To be perfectly frank with you, I don't know!' And it will be the truth, for he was simply an instrument in the hand of the enemy-a demon put those words in his mouth, and that was it!

Against Prayer

"You still don't like it? You are still resisting the idea? Then let's think about using prayer. Please tell me, when you set yourself to pray, to intercede, to really seek God's face (let's say when you plan to spend at least fifteen minutes), does everything go well? Are you able to concentrate your thoughts in prayer without problem? I bet not. Don't your thoughts wander? All of a sudden you think of a conversation you had, about an unfinished job, about something that happened six months ago. Let's analyze this together. Your thoughts were concentrated on God, right? You didn't have idle thoughts that were free to go looking for those things. So where did they come from? Isn't it obvious? It was demonic interference in your mind. Those extraneous thoughts don't have to be dirty or vile if our thoughts are diverted away from prayer then the enemy has achieved his objective.

"We need to understand something else about prayer. As soon as we start to pray we enter the spiritual sphere and with that the enemy gets busy. It is primarily in prayer that we wage spiritual war and the enemy feels a direct threat. So he goes into immediate action to distract us. You can put this down: no one remains alone when he prays—the moment you begin to pray in a serious way you will be 'covered' or opposed by at least one demon (depending on how dangerous the enemy thinks you are).

"This opposition may take various forms. If it isn't extraneous thoughts it is sleepiness. (When I was a boy we had a sure cure for insomnia. If I couldn't sleep my mother would say, 'Just pray and you'll go right to sleep.' Sure enough! I would start praying and in a few minutes I was snoring.) If it isn't sleepiness it's discouragement, or your mind goes blank or you feel fear. A homemaker finds a few moments and kneels to pray, and guess what happens. The telephone hasn't rung for a week but now it won't stop. She hasn't had any visitors for the longest time but at that exact moment the doorbell sounds. The children were playing quietly but all of a sudden a loud fight breaks out. If there are any dogs in the neighborhood I they all start barking. Isn't that so? Remarkable, don't you think? We are at war, my brothers!

Against Life

"The access that the enemy has to our minds can have drastic consequences. Consider the case of Ananias in Acts 5. Let's review the context. *'The multitude of those who believed were of one heart and of one soul; neither said any of them that any of the things which he possessed was his own; but they had all things common...Neither was there any among them that lacked; for as many as were possessors of lands or houses sold them, and brought the prices of the things that were sold and laid them down at the apostles' feet; and distribution was made unto every man according as he had need'* (Acts 4:32-35). That was the situation that gave rise to the case of Ananias. Please stop here and read Acts S:1-10.

After The Ambush

"As Peter explains, they didn't have to bring anything; or they could bring half, if they wished, as long as they didn't claim it was everything. Their problem was that they lied, wishing to receive credit as if they had brought the full amount. The apostle Peter affirms that it was Satan (again the proper name is used) who placed the idea in Ananias' mind, or heart. What was the result for Ananias? Death. Right? This is really heavy, people! A little later, in comes the wife: 'Is that the way it was, Sapphira?'

"That's right. Flop...she died on the spot! This access that the enemy has to our minds can result in physical death! Recall that he "had the power of death" and by bluffing (or usurping) he continues to do virtually as he pleases. I suspect that we might go into shock if we knew how many people have died as a direct result of demonic activity. But that's not the worst of it. Consider the case of Judas...

"In John 13:2 we read: *'Supper being ended, the devil having already put into the heart of Judas Iscariot, Simon's son, to betray him...'* While in John 13:27 we read: *'After supper Satan entered into him (Judas). Then Jesus said unto him, 'What you are going to do, do quickly.'* (Cf. Luke 22:3.) The idea of betraying Jesus was put in Judas' heart by the devil. But at the crucial moment Satan, by name, 'entered' into him, took control of him to guarantee that he would execute it. What was the result for Judas? Physical death, because a little later, overtaken by remorse (not repentance, which is different), he hanged himself. What further result did he receive? Spiritual death, because while praying to His own Father Jesus said, *'Those whom you gave me I have kept, and none of them is lost except the son of perdition, that the Scripture might be fulfilled'* (John 17:12). Note also Matthew 26:24: *'The Son of man goes as it is written of him, but woe unto that man by whom the Son of man is betrayed! It would have been good for that man if he had not been born.'* Judas was lost!

"The enemy's interference in peoples minds not only can result in physical death, it can also result in spiritual death. Judas isn't the only one. If it were just Judas per haps we could dismiss it—after all, Judas! Alas, no! We have already seen from 2 Corinthians 4:4 (also Mk. 4:15 and Lk. 8:12) that multitudes are going to hell as a result of Satan's interference in people's minds. (Since he is not omnipresent he works through a chain of command, using his angels, the demons.) This is a most serious matter—anything that results in the salvation of the soul, of the forfeiting of that salvation is of maximum importance. To close our eyes to this matter is treason against our King.

Other Evidences

"I know you still don't like it. Well, let's look at the Text some more. In 2 Corinthians 11:3 we are informed that 'the serpent (Satan) corrupts our minds;' in the context it is the minds of believers. That's the interference in our thoughts. In James 3:2-12 we find a very interesting description with respect to our thesis:

> 02 In many things we all stumble. If any man offend not in word the same is a perfect man, able also to bridle the whole body.
> 03 Behold, we put bits in the horses' mouths so that they may obey us, and we turn about their whole body.
> 04 Behold also the ships; though they are so great and are driven by fierce winds, yet are they turned about with a very small helm, wherever the pilot wills.
> 05 Even so the tongue is a little member and boasts great things. Behold how great a matter a little fire kindles!
> 06 The tongue also is afire, a world of iniquity; that is how the tongue is among our members, defiling the whole body and setting on fire

the whole course of our existence, being itself set on fire by hell.

07 For every kind of beast and bird, of reptile and marine animal can be tamed and has been tamed by mankind;

08 but the tongue can no man tame, incorrigible evil that it is, full of deadly poison!

09 Therewith bless we God, even the Father, and there with curse we men who are made in the likeness of God.

10 *Out of the same mouth proceed blessing and cursing. My brethren, these things ought not so to be.*

11 Does a spring send forth from the same opening both sweet water and bitter?

12 Can a fig tree, my brethren, yield olives, or a grapevine figs? Likewise no spring can give both salt water and fresh.

"We know that in nature a spring never gives both sweet and bitter water, alternately; it isn't possible. But lets imagine that one day we came across such a spring: one minute the water was sweet, the next it was bitter, and so on. How could we explain such a thing? There would have to two sources or veins feeding the spring, and they would have to meet just under the surface, taking turns. This is just what God's Word affirms happens with our mouth first blessing and then cursing proceed from them. Ho can this be? In fact, the language in verses 2, 6 and 8 could strike us as peculiar—not to offend in word is to a perfect; the tongue contaminates the body and inflames the course of life; the tongue is a fire, a world of iniquity, an incorrigible evil, a deadly poison! How can we explain such language? Whatever is going on? I believe that the answer may be found at the end of verse 6.

"What are we to understand when the Text says that the tongue 'is set on fire by hell'? At the very least it must mean that the tongue receives its capacity or ability t inflame from 'hell,' and therefore owes its inflammatory activity to 'hell.' But who or what is 'hell'? I believe this is an instance of metonymy (a figure of speech where word is used in place of another which is intimately associated with it). With whom is hell most closely associated? With Satan, since it has been prepared precisely for him and his angels (Mt. 25:41). I take it that this passage attributes a large share of the damage that results from the wrong use of the tongue to the activity of Satan and the demons, influencing the thinking and speaking of human beings. To be sure, we can make wrong use of our tongues all by ourselves, no doubt about it, but the language of the Text demands a further explanation. There are two sources contributing to our speech, our own will and malignant interference. Be not deceived!

"When you find yourself beside a stranger on a bus, train or plane, do you find it hard to converse with him? Say about the weather, fashions, politics or sports? Well, an introvert would presumably have difficulty, but most of us have little or no trouble. But if you shift the topic of conversation and start to talk about Jesus, then what happens? Do you speak as freely as you were? As a matter of fact this is not true. Correct? Don't you feel fear, get nervous, your mind goes blank; your palms get clammy? Why, do you suppose? Where does that fear come from? In 2 Timothy 1:7 we read: *'God has not given us a spirit of fear, but of power, of love and of self-control.'* It goes on to say, *'Therefore do not be ashamed of testifying to our Lord.'*

"The spirit of fear that attacks us when we want to witness about Christ does not come from God. The Text is clear. So where does it come from? Whose interest does it serve if we don't talk about Christ? Isn't it obvious? When a believer finds it hard to talk about Jesus, instead of calling him a coward and loading him with guilt we should first rebuke the spirit of fear. Obviously we can be cowards without demonic assistance. Still, you may be sure that many times we are attacked by an evil spirit. Then there are those terrible nightmares. The person feels that he is being suffocated. (Actually, 400 years ago the word 'nightmare' referred precisely to a demon that came and suffocated people while they slept.) If the demons can attack our minds while we are awake, how much more so while we are asleep and helpless protection). We must forbid any such interference before going to sleep; we can do this for others as well as for ourselves). Besides what happens in the mind, sometimes you can feel, or even see, an evil presence in the room. We are surrounded by the practice of spiritism of every sort (the criminal practices of Satanists are getting more and more attention in the news media; more and more movies deal with the occult. Go to the library of your local high school and just see how many books on occult practices are available to the students).

"The growing 'New Age' movement has significant components of spiritism; and converted spiritists/satanists declare that they have infiltrated our churches, our schools, the whole society to an alarming extent. It becomes hard to understand how there can be disciples of Jesus who still don't believe in the existence of the demons, and their activity, including an interference in our minds. I wouldn't be surprised if in a not too distant future the only people to remain skeptical about these things will be the members of certain Protestant churches. What a tragedy!"

—*Wilbur Pickering*

Epilogue

Epilogue

The Soldier's Challenge

As one of Satan's prisoners (P.O.W.) you were once bound up in an out-of-the-way cage somewhere. Out of the action and unable to escape the tethers that held you on your own power, you could not fight because of fear and bondage. You were *not* a target for the enemy to attack, instead Satan centered his attacks on those soldiers who escaped from his prison—Christians. They were set free by the power of the Holy Spirit—and they (we) are now his only threat. Since Christ's chosen soldiers are determined to set free all the captives Satan has in bondage, we pose a huge problem for him.

Yes, we are at war. It is a covert war; but a war nonetheless. Covert means that it is undercover, out of sight and out of mind. For the most part, it is an unseen war. When a slave-soldier from Satan's army is liberated and joins God's, he becomes like a beacon in a stormy, dark night. Satan is afraid the other captive soldiers may see His light in us and likewise be attracted to it. He sees the threat and lives in fear that he will lose more soldiers to God by them seeing your bright light. He will slander you; he will make you look unworthy because of the terrible things you have done in your past; and he will try to get you to turn back to your old ways so he can blackmail you. When all these things happen, your light can begin to draw dim. You may not feel worthy enough to even be called a Christian. (Sin does that—it makes us wary and hesitant of witnessing and proclaiming the name of Jesus).

This is psychological warfare at its best. I challenge you to get into the fight, be filled with the Holy Spirit, and go about the business of setting the captive free! Is it going to be easy? Is it going to be comfortable? No it isn't. Is it going to be rewarding? Absolutely! Let us be soldiers of the Cross as Jesus would have us be.

"You therefore must endure hardship as a good soldier of Jesus Christ. No one engaged in warfare entangles himself with the affairs of this life, that he may please him who enlisted him as a soldier" (2 Timothy 2:4).

Yielding

Without a doubt we are living in the very final days of the existence of mankind, and all that has been created on this earth according to God's plan. We are a people who have an opportunity to see our own history as we view the daily news and observe the activities that confirm the prophetic signs unfolding around us.

In this ministry to soldiers, that God so mercifully gave us, we must carefully consider, plan, and "re-think" our messages and direction of ministry. We must prepare to deliver to our brothers and help them change their conduct in these final hours of life in this world. If we are only in this to change and better ourselves, we have missed the boat. It is not about US…it is about Jesus. It is not "What would Jesus do?"….it is "Do What Jesus Did"!!!!

Always in the course of training soldiers there is a defining moment when each man or woman goes from the personal goal of "self-discipline" to the higher goal of "selflessness". I've always said that a veteran's true healing begins when he reaches the point that we turns from his own problems to assist someone else with theirs. When we can see that someone else may have a problem bigger than ours, and we need to help *them*—we become more effective troopers in the service for the Lord.

Soldiers and veterans of this world's wars are accustomed to suffering and hardship that few others ever know. If human suffering is essential for spiritual growth, then soldiers, who have borne the burdens of battle, certainly must possess a maturity level that goes beyond even their own awareness. (In most cases the suffering itself will be manifested as bitterness, hate and revenge until the soldier has surrendered as a born-again Christian.

Much is learned during times of pain and suffering that ordinarily would never be grasped if we had not experienced the "dark side" of a season in our lives. Not only does suffering cause spiritual growth but, it is the channel by which humans are introduced to the spiritual dimensions of their lives. Soldiers are in the business of suffering; we are veterans of despair and hardship, and it is through this suffering that I believe God is bringing us all closer to the refined image that He intended from the beginning.

There is one expectation that God has for us though, and if we do not heed, the refining process in our lives is severely diminished...and the time of suffering can be squandered. We may "mouth" the words and ideals of what we think is needed to be "clay" in the potter's hand, but are we really prepared to do the one thing that God requires of us? Are we ready and willing to *yield* to God's precise orders, according to His Word? Can we yield in spite of all our impulses to strike back, seek comfort, or run away? Can we be maligned, persecuted, beaten, or even put to death, without stepping out to take our own revenge? Are you willing to suffer some more, and be able to smile through the whole ordeal, without wanting to get some "pay back?" If you think this is impossible to do, let's see what God says about it. *"See that no one repays another with evil for evil but always seek after that which is good for one another and for all men. Rejoice always..."* 1 Thessalonians 5:15-16). Rejoice! Yes, God wants us to give thanks in all circumstances and to rejoice when bad things happen. (1 Thess. 5:18). This is powerful warfare—can you do it?

Those are some very tough, but serious questions for Soldiers who have dealt with adversity and enemies according to their earthly training, which has been by the swords and guns of this world. However, it is time for Christian soldiers who have been trained in earthly ways to begin thinking about how we will handle ourselves in the day of worldly crisis. Will it be by sword or spirit?

The Power of God

"When you do not have enough power, you are not weak enough." Jim Eliot–Martyred Missionary

It takes more self-control and strength to sit and wait for God than it does to step out and take matter into our hands. In spiritual warfare you must pay special attention to this and do everything possible not to get into your flesh; God's power is enough for every believer. However, our natures and conditioning make this a most difficult task.

We live in a society (in America) that was built on rugged individualism. Our forefathers, the pioneers and establishers of our country, took pride in being able to carve out the future for us with their bare hands and wit.

What Is The Eventual Crisis?

"And Jesus answered and said to them, "See to it that no one misleads you. For many will come in My name, saying, I am the Christ; and will mislead many. And you will be a hearing of wars and rumors of wars; see that you are not frightened, for those things must take place, but that is not let the end, for nation will rise against nation, and kingdom against kingdom, and in various places there will be famines and earth-

quakes. But all these things are merely the beginning birth pangs. Then they will deliver you to tribulation, and will kill you and you will be hated by all nations on account of My name. And at that time many will fall away and will deliver up one another and hate one another. And many false prophets will arise, and will mislead many. And because lawlessness is increased, most people's love will grow cold. But the one who endures to the end, he shall be saved (Matthew 24.4-137).

I present this to you...the suffering that you have endured has been a training ground to prepare you for these final days. You can either react to the coming persecution in the flesh, which is not God's way, or you can choose to persevere in the Spirit. You can choose to serve as a witness of faith, peace and love through Christ to those who are dying around you, and perhaps you may even be called upon to die for your faith, but will you continue your witness to a dying world by going peacefully, and *"giving thanks to God in all things"* (1 Thessalonians 5:18), or will you take up earthly arms and try to strike out in your own power?

I am not preaching unwarranted pacifism. I only want to know what God has to say about our conduct, and what He expects us to do when it all comes down. The Word of God clearly instructs us about Godly behavior. In these perilous times we must study these instructions and live accordingly, or we may find ourselves ensnared by our own "religious" rebellion.' We may find "our love growing cold", (Matthew 24:12), and we may *yield* to the world's ways instead of Gods.

What does the Bible say about how we are to behave and respond to the antagonism, violence and persecution that will come against us in our attempt to "endure to the end?" It is clear that God expects us to be perfect in these matters. "...*and make it your ambition to lead a quiet life and attend to your own business and work with your hands, just as we commanded you;*

so that you may behave properly toward outsiders and not be in any need" 1 Thessalonians 4:11-12.

I have heard many times, "well the Bible says 'an eye for an eye, a tooth for a tooth'; so it is apparently God's will for me to strike back in the same way that I'm being stricken." Exodus 21-24 does say something like that, but when Jesus came, things changed and He fulfilled the law. He also gave new instructions. *("You have heard that it was said, 'An eye for an eye, and a tooth for a tooth.' But I say to you, do not resist him who is evil; but whoever slaps you on your right cheek, turn to him the other also. And if anyone wants to sue you, and take your shirt, let him have your coat also. And whoever shall force you to go one mile, go with him two. Give him who asks of you, and do not turn away from him who wants to borrow from you. You have heard that it was said, 'You shall love your neighbor, and hate our enemy,' But I say to you, love your enemies, and pray for those who persecute you in order that you may be sons of your Father who is in heaven; for He causes the sun to rise on the evil and the good, and sends rain on the righteous and the unrighteous. For if you love those who love you, what reward have you? Do not even the tax gatherers do the same? And if you greet your brothers only, what do you do more than others? Do not even the Gentiles do the same? Therefore you are to be perfect, as your heavenly Father is perfect"* Matthew 5:38-48.

We must be diligent in our preparing to face the battles of the end days. We cannot go back to our old ways of using force against force. We must not resist because that is one of Satan's prime traps. One of the laws of physics is "What you resist, you become." Be diligent to prayerfully consider what your reactions may be to the violence and lawlessness that waits up ahead. You can do it your way, or you can do it God's way by yielding according to His Holy Word. It is a time, like no other, to surrender and abide in His plans and designs— not our own.

Section 3

8 Week Training Program

Welcome home...abide in it eternally.

To write a book like *After the Ambush* without providing a workbook section for application of the material in Section 1 and 2 is almost like leading someone to the Lord and then not further discipling them to a victorious life.

When studying, there is little value in just reading the "theory" of a subject. Much more is learned when we roll up our sleeves and do some "hands-on" work in the realm of what we are studying. "Doing" is the best part of "thinking." So, we have added this study guide section to help readers (as well as support groups) work through the spiritual warfare issues that challenge them day-to-day.

To obtain liberty from the oppressive aspects outlined in Sections 1 and 2, it is important to seek the Lord on how one should work through them in practical ways. He will be faithful to provide the tools of victory for us, and through the guidance of the Holy Spirit these tools will come alive in our hands.

After The Ambush

Group Interaction:

The following 8-week series of lessons are designed to help us break ungodly bonds, strengthen our walk with Christ, and prepare us to help set other captives free.

In a group setting the leader/facilitator will find these studies useful in establishing the focus for each meeting. They will also help keep attending veterans on the firing line and aiming at the correct targets as they are set free.

Ministries like Point Man are like evangelical "In and Out" medical processing centers. Here "triage" decisions are made and soldiers are brought to identify and discern their individual spiritual injuries. After the group leader (along with the other group members) helps a person identify specific areas that require prayer, they should be referred on for "specialty care" and "designer prayer". They need to be referred to the care and ongoing ministry of a pastor or eldership of a local church. However, the group facilitator should encourage the veteran to remain connected to the weekly meetings as a "volunteer" to help bring others out of the dark.

The Training Objective:

After the veteran becomes a volunteer to the call of arms at the meetings, he should be given marching orders that direct him to his next duty station (to his local church or mission field). He needs to go to this new duty station for the purpose of further instruction. This is called discipleship. The reason for this is to equip them to be fully dressed in God's armor and in a state of readiness to face the ministry of commanding their own life, and to be effective witnesses for the gospel. The effect of this witness should be so powerful that we inspire the unsaved to repent and seek the Father's forgiveness.

May you grow in the Lord and be led by the Holy Spirit through these weekly exercises.

Walking Point to Victory: A Study Guide

This section is the work of a joint effort by three Vietnam era veterans. Dana Morgan, the Executive Director of Point Man International Ministries, author Chuck Dean, and Dr. Joseph Owsiany, currently a missionary and medical doctor in Australia.

NOTE: It is important that each group member read Sections 1 & 2 before participating in these weekly lessons. The group leader/facilitator may want to make it a reading assignment before starting the group meetings; or read Sections 1 & 2 aloud in a group setting prior to any study.

Week 1

The Full Armor

"Put on the full armor of God that you may be able to stand *firm against the schemes of the devil"* (Ephesians 6:11).

Group reading:

Putting on the armor is crucial in our daily walk (and battles) as Christians. Many Christians do not take the time, or make the effort to pray on their armor on before starting each day. This usually lays them wide open to unnecessary pitfalls that the enemy (Satan and his hordes) constructs against them throughout each day. Many of these traps along the trail are directly connected to the curses, soul ties and other demonic activities we knowingly or unknowingly embraced while in S.E. Asia.

In Vietnam we never went on patrol without all our equipment and necessary items to survive combat. Through that experience, we all became keenly aware of the importance of being prepared and protected before entering critical situations. Being in God's army is no different, and He expects us to take up His armor daily to repel the assaults of our enemy. Being a good "Commander," He never sends His troops to the front lines without providing all the equipment they need. Ephesians 6:10-18 and Isaiah 58:8 is that equipment. I encourage you to study these scriptures (Ephesians 6:10-18, Isaiah 58:8) and memorize them. Then make it a daily discipline to put the full armor of God on in prayer. Here is an example of how to do that:

"I put on the belt of truth, that today I speak and hear only the truth of God.

"I put on the breastplate of righteousness, that my heart is protected by God. I wear it to have a right standing before God and His throne today.

"I shod my feet with the gospel of peace, that everywhere I step God's peace will abound.

"I take up the shield of faith to ward off the fiery darts of the enemy. Jesus, I proclaim that You are my shield; a shield that I can kneel down behind and seek protection from the enemy

"I put on the helmet of salvation, that my mind will be protected by God. Lord, transform my mind into the mind of Christ this day, that all thoughts that I have would be the thoughts of Jesus Himself.

"I take up the Sword of the Spirit, the Word of God, to wield against the enemy in time of warfare. I also pray that this Sword may be used to circumcise my own fleshly heart and to give me strength this day to rise above the sin that abounds always in my life and in this world.

"Lord, I thank You for protecting my back with Your glory as proclaimed in Isaiah 58:8. The Lord God almighty is my rearguard, and I do not

have to be afraid of what is behind me. I refuse
evil and choose *good* just as Jesus did. Today, I
refuse the will of Satan and choose the will of
God!"

It is very important not to make this some sort of ritual
that we just give "lip service" to. Vain incantations will get us
nowhere, and further away from the will of God than we want
to be. Each part of the armor that we verbally call upon ourselves is to make a determined effort to actually put on and
wear them as a part of a daily practice. Now you can proceed
from "theory" to "practical" and *apply* the Word to your life.

Exercise 1

The Belt of Truth:

Truth is a precious asset to have. It is where we find trust,
and for veterans who have lost their trust of people and sys-
tems, it becomes even more valuable.

The belt used on clothing in Christ's time was a device
which not only held the robe gathered at the waist, but it was
hollow as well. It was used as a money belt, which covered
the belly and it guarded against theft within the man's protected reach.

It is interesting to see this relationship between money
and truth (or trust). Money represents a high degree of faith—
it is a form of confidence that we share in our business trans-
actions. If I was to give you a sack of potatoes and in ex-
change you give me three dollars, I have to believe that your
currency has enough value for me to buy something with it.
Your money represents a form of truth to me that keeps our
relationship in good standing. If it is a lie (or counterfeit), it
is doubtful that we will continue with any further transac-
tions. We have become separated relationally, and this gives
place for us to sin against one another.

After The Ambush

Determine the truth in all matters by seeking Holy Spirit guidance. His number one job is to point us to Jesus the Son, Who is the way, the truth and the life. By doing what Jesus did (DWJD), we find an accurate way to put on the Belt of Truth each day.

Putting on the Belt of Truth, however, is not just saying meaningless words representing truth—it is an *act* of acquiring and maintaining the truth in everything we do. This keeps the Word of God within the protected reach of our arms. A person cannot keep what he does not acquire. Therefore a man wearing the belt of truth must be prepared to both acquire and keep the truth at all costs, just as he would also do for any worldly treasure. To fail to do so may cause his money belt to be emptied, and his belly to bloat.

Salvation comes by grace alone, but truth comes only by drawing close to God— Who is the truth. Moses climbed several mountains to reach God as Christ also did when He withdrew into the wilderness to pray. This is hard work requiring diligence and disciplined effort. It is one reason the men of God are called mighty.

By drawing close to God we are shown more and more of the truth.

(TDR) Training/Discussion Routine:

1. What is truth?
2. How does a lie loosen, or weaken, your belt of truth?
3. When did truth prevail in one of your experiences that made a difference?

Exercise 2

The Breastplate of Righteousness

Many believe the armor that the Apostle Paul was talking about in Ephesians 6 was fashioned after the Roman armor of the day. This is not so. It was patterned after the Hebrew armor of the Old Testament times. The breastplate is not a piece of body armor. It is rather a garment worn criss-crossed over our chests. It is specifically designed for us to carry close to our hearts the needed character qualities, which are essential in helping us discern the will of God.

The heart represents the throne of God. The breastplate garment is worn over this area to help us draw close to His throne for the purposes of securing God's justice and right judgment. When we do this we dispel the darkness brought on by lies of the unjust who speak "oppression and revolt" (the works of the enemy).

Wearing and applying the breastplate of righteousness gives us the opportunity to reflect the fact that we are justified people who declare justice in the name of Jesus Christ.

TDR) Training/Discussion Routine:

1. What injustice about Vietnam has embittered your heart?
2. How have you acted out that bitterness?
3. Ask for and receive prayer for healing your heart.

The Boots of Peace

God directs the paths of our feet. (Psalms 17:5 "*My steps have held fast to your paths, my feet have not slipped. 6 I have called upon thee, for thou*

*wilt answer me, O God: Incline your ear unto me,
and hear my speech..."*

The Hebrew and Greek words for "shod" mean to bind or to lock. The Apostle Paul's reference in Eph 6:15 is a command to bind the feet with the "readiness" to proclaim the Gospel of peace. The goal of proclaiming the Gospel of Peace is not merely speaking forth, but also recognizes the Father and subsequently establishes His Kingdom by doing His will. We must "walk" out what we are proclaiming, and we walk by faith, not by sight (2 Corinthians 5:7). This is a true "point man"...a soldier who can step out in faith and act not according to what he "sees", but by having faith knowing that God is ordering each step.

Meditation on this and many scriptures about "feet" (Ps 18:33, Ps 25:15, Ps 31:9, Ps 40:2, Ps 119: 59, 101, 105, Pr. 26:6, Pr 4:26), reveals that it is God who directs us, so that we subsequently walk in confidence, not slipping into the hands of the enemy of our souls. We are to order our ways and make straight paths for our feet (Heb 12:13).

In the physical, natural law states that for every action there is a reaction. Likewise, spiritually, for every action good or bad, there is a consequence, what happened to us in Vietnam is an example of what we find in scripture.

It is better not to make a vow than to make a vow and not fulfill it. Do not let your mouth lead you into sin. (Ecc. 5:5-6). We went to Vietnam originally to "stop the spread of communism", help those that could not defend themselves, and other lofty goals. The reality soon became obvious that there was no plan to win the war, and in so doing we lost our purpose (in a sense we were abandoned).

Even though God ordains all governments (Romans 13), ours was not led by God—but was allowed to proceed by God. As soldiers, we became a test lab for theories, new equipment, tactics and so on. As children many of us were brought up in mainline denominational churches and were taught to honor those in authority. We saw nothing wrong with going to war as a reflection of our national values and our duty before God.

What happened was an entirely different scenario. We lost our moral compass and our support for our core values here in this country and the effects spilled into RVN. What we saw in RVN was a reflection of the times here in the USA. Question all authority, anyone over thirty was the enemy, God is dead and so on. Eat, drink, and be merry became the order of the day.

There were many vocal and highly visible individuals that seemed to parrot and promote this malaise and received all the media attention. They were spiritually blinded. The scripture says that God gave them over to their lusts (which doesn't mean just sex). Mainstream clergy, politicians and the general public remained virtually silent. It is not my intent to comment on the political rightness or justify the war. Deep, deep divisions remain to this day over the war and its conduct.

The Gospel of Peace is what you need to wrap yourself in. When you got saved you received Jesus. He is resident within you. Speak peace and life into whatever situation you find yourself in wherever you go. Remember there is no peace without Jesus.

TDR) Training/Discussion Routine:

1. What is the gospel of Peace?
2. How do I speak life into a situation?
3. What does speaking peace and life mean?
4. Can you identify a time in RVN where the opposite occurred? How has it affected you today?

The Shield of Faith

The shield (thureos) used by the Israelites was a large oblong shield. It was called a scuta, which meant that it looked like a **door** (thura) and it was made of wood and covered with hides. In the Scriptures it is mentioned figuratively of God and of earthly princes as the defenders of their people (Gen. 15:1; Deut. 33:29; Ps. 33:20; 84:11). Jesus, as the Prince of Peace, is certainly our shield.

The faith placed in us by the Holy Spirit is compared to a shield (Eph. 6:16). When we commit, in faith, to kneel our spirits down behind Jesus and allow Him to protect us in all circumstances, we remain unscathed by the fiery missiles of the devil.

Shields in biblical times were always "anointed" with oil, (Isaiah 21:5 *They prepare the table, they set the watch, they eat, they drink: rise up, ye princes, anoint the shield.*). This was done in order to preserve them, and at the same time make the missiles of the enemy glide off them more easily. Jesus is the Holy and anointed one, and our faith in Him as Savior, Deliverer, and Lord keeps us from being destroyed—as long as we do not get out in front of Him in our activities.

When Jesus said that He is the way, the truth and the life, He proclaimed that He is not only our point man who leads the way, but He desires to stay out in front of us as well. He is our "**door**" and exercising the faith that He has put in us protects us.

John 10:7 *Jesus therefore said unto them again, Verily, verily, I say unto you, **I am the door** of the sheep. 8 All that came before me are thieves and robbers: but the sheep did not hear them. 9 **I am the door**; by me if any man enter in, he shall be saved, and shall go in and go out, and shall find pasture. 10 The thief comes so that he may steal, and kill, and destroy: I came that they may have life, and may have it abundantly. 11 I am the good shepherd: the good shepherd lays down his life for the sheep.*

TDR) Training/Discussion Routine:

1. What "doors" (other than Jesus) have you tried to hide behind for protection?
2. How can you step out in faith? What does that mean?

The Helmet of Salvation

> "For who among men knows the things of a man, except the spirit of the man, which is in him? Even so the things of God no one knows, except the Spirit of God. But we did not receive the spirit of the world, but the spirit, which is from God; that we might know the things that were freely given to us by God. These things also we speak, not in words which man's wisdom teaches, comparing spiritual things with spiritual. But the natural man cannot see the things of the Spirit of God: for they are foolishness to him; and he cannot know them, because they are spiritual in nature. But he who is spiritual judges all things, and he himself is judged of no man. For 'Who has known the mind of the Lord, that he may instruct him?' But we have the mind of Christ" 1 Corinthians 2:11-16.

When we pray on, or "take", the Helmet of Salvation, a deep spiritual course of action is initiated. We are doing two things:

1. First we are making the effort required to be transformed from a man of the earth to a man of the heavenlies. At that moment we decide, *by our will*, to have the mind of Christ by wearing His helmet of salvation. When it is worn with sincerity and wisdom we submit to our supreme authority (God) and He then shows us the world through His eyes and not our natural ones. We then have the mind of Christ as we go about our day. (1 Corinthians 2:11-16).

2. Secondly, when we fit the Helmet of Salvation upon our heads we make a declaration to the enemy that we are men and women under authority. (*"Now when Jesus entered Capernaum, a centurion came to him, pleading with Him, saying, 'Lord, my servant is lying at home paralyzed, dreadfully tormented.' And Jesus said to him, 'I will come and heal him.' And the centurion answered and said, 'Lord, I am not worthy that You should come under my roof; but only say the word, and my servant shall be healed. For I also am a man under authority, having soldiers under me. And I say to this one, go, and he goes; and to another, come, and he comes; and to my servant, do this, and he does it.' And when Jesus heard it, He marveled, and said to those who followed, 'Assuredly, I say to you, I have not found such great faith, not even in Israel'"* Matthew 8:5-10.)

Multitudes of Vietnam veterans have an "authority problem". One major cause of this was poor leadership from White House to war zone during that era. It has been a central issue in need of healing for many decades now.

As Christian veterans we must deal with the "authority issue" if we expect to receive our healing and help others with theirs. Putting on the Helmet of Salvation is not just a ritual of words that we pray, but we follow up with action by submitting ourselves to spiritual authority as well. We must be accountable to God's appointed church government, wherever they are joined to His Body. This is no different than an army's active organization from General Staff down to Cook, KP, and picking up cigarette butts on police call. The executive heads are outlined in Ephesians 4:11 (*"...And He Himself gave some to be apostles, some prophets, some evangelists, and some pastors and teachers."*).

This command structure (ordained by Jesus Himself) is active in the Body today, whether or not current leadership recognize or acknowledge it. These leaders are accountable to one another and ultimately to Christ. When they are recognized and allowed to function in their offices and giftings we have a living dynamic body, where the fruit of the Spirit and God's power is manifest. Our Helmet of Salvation is coming under the umbrella of God's appointed authority, and this is wisdom and the mind of Christ.

TDR) Training/Discussion Routine:

1. Why does the natural man disqualify himself spiritual matters?
2. Who is your spiritual authority? How have you submitted yourself, your family and your ministry to him (them)?

The Sword of the Spirit

> *"For the word of God is living, and active, and sharper than any two-edged sword, and piercing even to the dividing of soul and spirit, of both joints and marrow, and quick to discern the thoughts and intents of the heart"* Hebrews 4:12.

The Word of God is like a two edged sword...rightly dividing. It is the *sword* that we wield not only against our enemies, but we use it daily to carve away any of our own flesh that Satan can take advantage of and use against us. In the beginning was the Word, and the Word was with God, and the Word was God. He was with God in the beginning. Through him all things were made; without Him nothing was made that has been made. In Him was life, and that life was the light of men. The light shines in the darkness, but the darkness has not overcome it. (John 1:1-4)

So here we are, carrying the Word of God. Scripture says that Jesus is the Word. He is seated, however, at the right hand of the Father, but the Holy Spirit, the Counselor and Comforter, has the duty of teaching us all things, and leading us to Jesus.

Wielding this sword is a responsibility not to be taken lightly. All the pieces of the armor work in conjunction with each other. For example, without the mind of Christ we would not have any clue as to the proper use of the sword. We would not be able to discern or cut through the onslaught of the devil. This is the sword that cuts through the darkness of our lives and exposes those areas that need cleaning out. The sword is light and Jesus is the light of the world—and has overcome all.

Use the Sword of the Spirit to light up and cut out those areas of flesh that we have not given fully over to the Lord and get on with our lives. Let the past finally be past at last.

TDR) Training/Discussion Routine:

1. How does the Sword of the Spirit...the Word of God...help us have the mind of Christ?
2. How does the Sword of the Spirit help us fight Satan? How does carving our own flesh with it defeat Satan?

Week 2

Hour 1—Identifying the Correct Enemy

Believe it or not, no man or woman on earth is your enemy. They may be used by the real enemy to irritate and upset you, but they are *not* the enemy. The true enemy uses people as smoke screens to conceal his covert activities against our lives. So why do we think other humans are the enemy? It is because we can see and touch them, and they become the most "logical" targets for our troubles. When we directly attack people we are fighting in darkness—and the enemy always wins a war fought in the dark. We must use illumination flares on the battlefield and shine the light of the gospel truth of Jesus Christ on all enemy activities.

So who is this enemy?

When we are doing spiritual warfare, we are fighting against Satan's agents (spirits or fallen angels). Satan is not omnipresent and he cannot be everywhere, so he dispatches demons to do the job. These demons conduct covert operations almost in every case. They would rather have us shooting at each other rather than at them. The communists in Vietnam had a similar strategy to the one Satan fights us with today.

The communist army primarily used guerilla warfare because they were outgunned and technologically disadvantaged to fight the allies. Therefore, they chose to use hit-and-run tactics, small unit actions, and to wear us down so we could be caught off guard. They avoided direct contact (conventional) combat as much as possible.

Here are some ways the communist Vietnamese fought against us. As you read you will see how these methods match Satan's ways in fighting us in the spirit realm. You will also notice how closely they parallel Satan's forces as they engage us in combat. These are classic examples of how a covert war is similar both in the physical and spiritual:

1) The VC attempted to look as much like the civilian population as possible. (Satan disguises himself and can even look like a friend—an "angel of light".)

2) The VC did not fight for physical territory. They fought to win the hearts and minds of people. (If Satan can shift our attention, our zeal, our time, our hearts and our minds onto something other than Jesus and the Great Commission, he has won. We have fallen into idolatry without even knowing it. He has captured our heart and mind, leaving us unfruitful and ineffective in the Kingdom of God.)

3) The VC deployed booby traps along trails to destroy our confidence. Maiming and killing our buddies along the march weakened our morale and desire to keep fighting. We were taking casualties but never saw the enemy. After the explosives were detonated the enemy could watch their destruction from afar—out of harm's way. (Satan knows he cannot win the war. However, if he can set enough traps along our

walk to make us hurt, and be unsure of our faith, then he can keep us from being effective witnesses for Christ. He usually wreaks enough misery from a distance that we tend to forget who the real adversary is. Many times we target each other as the enemy because he...the devil...does not appear to be an obvious player in the whole scenario).

4) The VC used innocent civilians, even to the point of destroying them, as decoys to undermine our security and confidence. It was a common practice to strap explosive charges on small children and send them into groups of G.I.s to make friends and win their affection. When the child would get close enough, the communist soldier would detonate the charge with a remote switch, taking out the G.I.s—and the child. (Often Satan will use even good things to win our affections. Once he has accomplished this, he ambushes us and attempts to destroy us).

5) The VC tried to get us to mistakenly kill our fellow warriors. One particular tactic he used was what we called "cutting the pie." At night, when we would stop daylight operations in the jungle, we would dig into night-defensive positions. The entire unit formed into a large circle (a pie shape) for protection. Normally there were two men to a hole, and one slept while the other kept watch for enemy activity. The VC would probe a point in the perimeter circle, making a lot of noise to attract attention, and would try to take a slice out of the "pie." After making the noise they would pull back into the jungle and hope we would fire our weapons in the direction of the noise—which would be at our own men on the other side of the circle. (Satan deploys the same strategy against us. He creeps into our midst and causes disruptive "noise", and then pulls back into his jungle to wait for us to kill one another. He tries his best to cause fights, quarrels, dissatisfaction and dissension in our midst. All the while he has distanced himself and remains the undetected source of trouble. This tactic is evident in almost every church fellowship in Christendom. Most pastors can attest to this.

6) The VC attempted to stay *close* to U.S. military units. They knew that the closer they could be to us, especially in a firefight, the less likely it was that we would call in artillery or air support, in fear of directing the incoming fire on ourselves. (Satan sends his forces against us in the same manner. He gets as close to us as possible so we cannot determine which direction to call in "air support" to take him out. Many times he is so close we completely overlook him when he is in our midst.

TDR) Training/Discussion Routine:

1. What is Satan's mission against people?
2. How does Satan use our misdirected targets against people to accomplish his mission?
3. Discuss ways and examples of how situations in life are smoke screens for enemy activity

Hour 2—Binding and Loosing the Enemy

> *"But no one can enter into the house of the strong man, and steal his property, unless he first bind the strong man; and then he will spoil his house"*
> Mark 3:27

The souls of men are the "property" of the strong man (Satan) in Mark 3:27. Satan doesn't have any need for your Mercedes Benz, home, gold, silver, or any other material possession, all he wants to do is take us to hell with him when it is all over. We need to not only walk in our freedom from hell, but it is our commission as Christian soldiers to snatch the lost from his hands as well. We are instructed in that same Scripture (Mark 3:27) to move into action and take that "property" by binding the enemy and loosing his grip from the hearts of the lost. Evangelism…bringing the lost to salvation…finds its heart in the midst of Mark 3:27. It is a simple, but powerful, means of warfare to liberate the oppressed.

When we are doing spiritual warfare, we are fighting against Satan's agents (spirits or fallen angels) dispatched to harass and harm us. We are not fighting him directly! I believe it is fair to say that when we bind and loose, we must bind and loose the demon assigned to cause the problems. This gives us much more accuracy in our firepower against the *"...rulers, powers, world forces of this darkness, and spiritual forces of wickedness in the heavenly places"* (Ephesians 6:12).

Some people say that it is necessary to know every demon by name, but this is a false and deceptive notion from the enemy to weaken your strategy and distract you. In Vietnam, we certainly didn't have to know the name of every Viet Cong soldier before we decided to shoot at them—and they certainly didn't know our names. We just met on the battlefield and engaged each other in combat. No introductions were necessary. It's the same here. However, if the Lord does reveal the identity or name of a specific demon, your warfare will be much more effective if you call it by name (see Mark 5:9). It is important to realize that even though you don't necessarily need to know the name of every demon in a combat situation, it is best do seek the Lord for discernment in detecting what kind of demon it is.

TDR) Training/Discussion Routine:

1. In regards to binding and loosing, what did Jesus mean when He prayed in Matthew 6:10 *"Your kingdom come, Your will be done on earth as it is in heaven"*?
2. Why is the Name of Jesus your best weapon in binding and loosing?

Week 3

Freedom from Anger — Victory over the Curses

(Note: It is recommended that the video message from Pastor S.M. Davis *"Victory Over the Spirit of Anger"* be viewed prior to this session. It can be ordered by calling his ministry toll-free number — 1-800-500-8853.)

When we have the "spirit of anger" people walk on egg-shells around us—and even though we haven't done anything outwardly to give them reason to be afraid us, they are almost terrorized at the thought of upsetting us. We can have a smile on our faces and do kind things, but we still may be emitting a "feeling" that if someone screws up around us we will be the first to condemn or chastise them for their mistake. If this is happening to you, then you have the "spirit of anger," and you need to deal with it.

Ephesians 4:31 clearly states that God expects us to put away all anger from our lives (*"…let ALL wrath and anger be put away from you."*). We must do this to be his best soldier. I believe controlling our anger is a major key, and necessary ingredient, to breaking permanently free from the curses put on Vietnam veterans by those Buddhist monks.

Curses are activated through the spoken word. The Scriptures tell us that words are not mere sounds on the lips; but life and death are in the power of the tongue. Words are agents sent forth for good or bad—for us, or for others. (Read about the blessings and curses in Deuteronomy 27-30, and when Jesus cursed the fig tree in Mark 11).

Have you ever seen a person get prayed for over and over again for the same problem? When people cannot get free, there is always a reason. Sometimes it is due to disobedience and lack of submission to God, but many have this happen because of curses that have never been broken. They need to be broken by the power of the name and shed blood of Jesus

Christ of Nazareth. If this doesn't happen, these people will continue to be defeated.

Curses act as shields and fences around demon spirits. These evil spirits can be invoked to manifest during ministry, but they will not and cannot come out until the curses have been discovered (discerned) and then broken.

TDR) *Training/Discussion Routine:*

1. Ask each group member to talk about what part of the culture or Asian traditions they agreed with, participated in, or how they gave up pieces of sovereignty to foreign gods and unseen forces.
2. Invite all attendees to be prayed for and break the curse of "anger", and then the curse of "no peace", and lastly the curse of "wandering". (Pray the warfare prayers in Section 2).
3. Recommend and discuss accountability with one another on the issue of anger. Encourage openness in admitting anger when it happens and work out an accountable *price* that needs to be paid to help each member control the spirit of anger. (Note: This is not to be construed as a form of "works" as a way to "repent" of your anger…but is merely a method of disciplining ourselves so as to bring anger under control.)

Week 4

Yielding to God — The New Code of Conduct

There is one expectation that God has for us in His army, and if we do not heed, the refining process in our lives is severely diminished. We may "mouth" the words and ideals of what we think is needed to be "clay" in the potter's hand, but are we really prepared to do the one thing that God requires of us? Are we ready and willing to *yield* to God's precise orders, according to His Word? Can we yield in spite of all our impulses to strike back, seek comfort, or run away? Can we be maligned, persecuted, beaten, or even put to death, without stepping out to take our own revenge? Are you willing to suffer some more, and be able to smile through the whole ordeal, without wanting to get some "pay back?" If you think this is impossible to do, let's see what God says about it. *"See that no one repays another with evil for evil but always seek after that which is good for one another and for all men. Rejoice always..."* 1 Thessalonians 5:15-16. Rejoice! Yes, God wants us to give thanks *in* all circumstances, and to rejoice when bad things happen. (1 Thess. 5:18). This is powerful warfare—can you do it?

Those are some very tough, but serious, questions for soldiers who have dealt with adversity and enemies according to their earthly training. We have all been trained to deal with such difficulty by means of the swords and guns of this world. However, it is time for the Christian soldiers (who have been trained in earthly ways) to begin thinking about how we will handle ourselves in the day of worldly crisis. Will it be by sword or spirit?

Here is a Christian Code of Conduct written expressly for Point Man Ministries:

"Submit therefore to God. (then) *Resist the devil and he will flee from you"* James 4:7.

The Code of Conduct for a Soldier of Christ

Article I

I am one of God's fighting men. I walk by faith, not by sight. I conduct myself in a manner worthy of the Gospel of Christ. I will do nothing from empty conceit; but with humility of mind regard others as more important than myself.

After The Ambush

I serve the Lord, my God, and none other. I realize that no soldier in active service entangles himself in the affairs of daily civilian pursuits (i.e., man's politics, worldly concerns that are perishing). He does this in order that he may please only God, who enlisted him (2 Tim. 2:4).

Article II

I surrender of my own free will to the Lord, my God. If in command I will surrender my men to the Him, and strive to lead them in a way so that Jesus may take them all captive. After becoming a captive of Christ, I will never resist Him in any way. I will make no effort to escape. I will accept no favors from the enemy.

Article III

If I become a prisoner of war, I will make every effort to escape and aid others in escaping. I will resist Satan by submitting to Jesus Christ, my Lord and Savior. I will obey only the lawful orders of Jehovah God, and His canonized Scriptures. When questioned I will always be ready to give witness to the hope and glory of the Gospel of Christ to set the captives free.

Article IV

While fighting in God's army I will always remember that my fight is not against flesh and blood, but against the rulers and powers of the darkness of this world. I will condition myself to the proper utilization of the Word of God in all my battles. I will pray unceasingly as a means of warfare, and do all things without grumbling and complaining. I will strive to be a light to the world.

Article V

I will fit myself in the full armor of God every day . I will never attempt to do warfare without my armor being in place. (Ephesians 6)

Article VI

I will let love be without hypocrisy, abhorring evil, cling-ing to good. I am devoted to others in brotherly love. I am diligent in praying for others, contributing to the needs of my fellow soldiers, and practicing hospitality. I choose to bless those who persecute me, and will not curse them. I rejoice with those who rejoice and weep with those who weep. I will never pay back evil for evil to anyone. I respect what is right in the sight of all men. I will never take my own revenge, and if my enemy is hungry, I will feed him; if he is thirsty I will give him something to drink. I will not allow myself to be overcome by evil.

Article VII

I will dispense true justice, and practice kindness and com-passion for my brothers. I will never oppress the widow or orphan, the stranger or the poor, and I will never devise evil in my heart against another.

Article VIII

I will apply all diligence in my faith to supply moral ex-cellence, knowledge, self-control, perseverance, godliness, brotherly kindness, and love to those around me, thereby ensuring that the entrance to the heavenly kingdom will be abundantly supplied to them all.

Article IX

I will love the Lord God with all my heart, soul and might. His words will always be on my heart. I will teach them to my sons and fellow soldiers. His words will always be bound in my heart and I will write them on my doorposts and gates.

Article X

I will never forget that I am one of God's fighting men, responsible for my actions, and dedicated to the principles, which make men free through the salvation of the Lord Jesus Christ. I will trust in my God forever.

…Amen.

TDR) *Training/Discussion Routine:*

1. Why is a code of conduct needed in an army?
2. How is God's code of conduct different than man's?

Week 5

The Suffering Soldier — A Way of War

Pain and suffering lead us to deeper wells of "living water". It is through hardship that our spiritual lives are stretched to new dimensions, because we see more clearly how much we need Jesus' help. Probably few others experience the levels of hardship that a soldier does when he is at war. For this reason, I say that veterans are probably fine candidates for becoming some of the world's most anointed and gracious ministers and missionaries.

I once read how the grapes in the Bordeaux regions of France are akin to the veterans of the Vietnam War. In Bordeaux some of the finest wine is made, and it is because the vines on which the grapes are grown have had to endure rough, arid ground to produce their fruit. The French call it "the suffering of the vine".

The vintners plant vines on rocky, dry hillsides and it seems that nothing can grow there. But the vine's root system eventually reaches tap water, and the plant begins to grow into the hardiest of species—producing some of the finest grapes and award-winning wine in the world. The plant became resilient and strong by enduring the struggle of finding a source that gave it life. In the same way veterans who find Jesus, find the living water that sustains them and causes them to become the finest instruments in the Vintner's hand. (*"...Jesus answered and said to her, 'If you knew the gift of God, and who it is that says to you, 'Give Me a drink'; you would have asked him, and He would have given you living water.' The woman said to him, 'Sir, you have nothing to draw with, and the well is deep: where then do you get this living water? Are you greater than our father Jacob, who gave us the well, and drank from it himself, and his sons, and his livestock?' Jesus answered and said to her, 'Whoever drinks of this water will thirst again, but whoever drinks of the water that I shall give him will never thirst. But the water that I shall give him shall become in him a fountain of water springing up into everlasting life'"* John 4:10-14.)

If you have ever seen the old-fashioned winemakers stomp and crush the grapes to make wine, you know that to be fruit in God's vat we will be called to endure some hardship. But it is all for good reason...God wants to ferment the finest wine by squeezing us until we pour out the essence He has put in us through the "living waters".

> *"Suffer hardship with me, as a good soldier of Christ Jesus. No soldier in service entangles himself in the affairs of this life; that he may please him who enlisted him as a soldier"* 2 Timothy 2:3-4.

It is a costly commission. It costs us our lives as we begin to live for Him and no longer for ourselves.

TDR) Training/Discussion Routine:

1. Why do our spiritual dimensions expand through suffering?
2. Why do veterans make good ministers or missionaries?

Week 6

Airstrikes — Fighting from our Knees

When God's soldiers pray they are, in essence, on a direct commo line to God. In Vietnam we called for close air support, artillery, or naval bombardments when we could not break contact with overpowering enemy forces. Now we call God for "airstrikes" when we are troubled, or in need. In spiritual warfare it is essential to study, train, and exercise our prayer life.

Prayer is a mystery. It is a physical action that we do in the physical realm to get things to happen in the spiritual. It is our doorway of speaking from one universe into another, and we don't have to direct these requests, praises, thanksgiving, etc. through a chain of command...they go directly from us to the Supreme Commander in heaven. He hears them all. What a privilege to serve in such an army!

Prayer is the intercourse of our soul with God. When we can pour out our soul before the Lord (1 Sam. 1:15) it is *the* romance that He desires to have with us, and in prayer we draw near to God (Ps. 73:28) like lovers anticipating one another.

When God's people pray, things get done. Here are some examples of that:

Abraham's servant prayed to God, and God directed him to the person who should be wife to his master's son and heir (Gen. 24:10-20).

Jacob prayed to God, and God inclined the heart of his irritated brother, so that they met in peace and friendship (Gen. 32:24-30; 33:1-4).

David prayed, and God defeated the counsel of Ahithophel (2 Sam. 15:31; 16:20-23; 17:14-23).

Daniel prayed, and God enabled him both to tell Nebuchadnezzar his dream and to give the interpretation of it (Dan. 2: 16-23).

Nehemiah prayed, and God inclined the heart of the king of Persia to grant him leave of absence to visit and rebuild Jerusalem (Neh. 1:11; 2:1-6).

Esther and Mordecai prayed, and God defeated the purpose of Haman, and saved the Jews from destruction (Esther 4:15-17; 6:7, 8).

The believers in Jerusalem prayed, and God opened the prison doors and set Peter at liberty, when Herod had resolved upon his death (Acts 12:1-12).

Paul prayed that the thorn in the flesh might be removed, and his prayer brought a large increase of spiritual strength, while the thorn perhaps remained (2 Cor. 12:7-10).

Prayer is like the dove that Noah sent out of the Ark. It blessed him not only when it returned with an olive-leaf in its mouth, but when it never returned at all Noah had to relinquish it to God. When we pray our prayers we must be willing to let God have them, and if we never see them return in our lifetime, never fear...they will be answered.

Our primary weapon, the Name of Jesus, ("If you ask anything in My name, I will do it." John 14:14), is at the heart of our warfare. By invoking the Name of Jesus in our prayers against the dark forces that surround us we step out in faith that the Word of God is true...and He is faithful to deliver what we ask. In prayer, we punctuate the thrust of our swords with the name above all names...Jesus Christ of Nazareth.

TDR) Training/Discussion Routine:

1. What is a prayer life?
2. How do you develop a prayer life?
3. Why is a prayer life (beyond ritual mechanical prayer) critical to our walk?

Week 7

Search and Discovery: Looking for Holes in our Perimeter

We all have blind spots, and we all have sin. To claim that we have arrived and we have no sin destroys our credibility and shows a weak character (*"If we say that we have no sin, we deceive ourselves, and the truth is not in us."* 1 John 1:8). Therefore, it is most important to walk in the light with not only ourselves, but with the world around us. It is a matter of honor.

When every part of our life is exposed to the light, and we are transparent in our doings, the enemy suffers one of his most crushing defeats. It is only when we harbor unconfessed sins and ungodly practices does Satan own us. These dark, secret areas of our lives are the holes in our perimeter. The enemy is looking for the holes so he can rush in and disrupt our lives and our work for God. We must learn to spot the holes and repair them immediately.

One of the important aspects of a support group setting is that we can be humans that fail and still be accepted by the others. Do you know why? Because all of us are far from perfect, and all stumble along the way. We need one another, but most of all we need to know that each of us are weak vessels and subject to fail at any moment. We are together because we recognize that in each other, and we commit to being there for the other person without evaluating or judging what is spoken at a time of confessional sharing. This is why it is so important to let Christ's light shine into our dark places...we must see one another and allow others to see us as well. Anything less is hypocrisy and unacceptable in God's army.

Confession has had a bad rap for many years by Protestant Christians. Most have seen confession used to manipulate people and squander the purpose of repentance by other types of Christian persuasions (i.e. Catholicism). But this is a classic case of "throwing the baby out with the bathwater." Confession is a very scriptural part of our growing and healing.

"Confess your sins one to another, and pray for one another, that you may be healed." James 5:16. This scripture is not only talking about healing from physical ailments, it is also speaking of the wounds in our psyche and the things in our past that we fear would shame us. To keep our shameful deeds hidden and unconfessed only make us more vulnerable targets for Satan. He waits to control us and keep us in his grip by what we hold in secret.

Our priorities can be useful to God, or useful to Satan. Part of our commission is to use spiritual eyes to discern the ways of God (and His warnings). When we have His eyes we can effectively "walk point" for those who do not have these eyes. (*But the natural man cannot see the things of the Spirit of God: for they are foolishness to him; and he cannot know them, because they are spiritual in nature.* 1 Corinthians 2). If we fail to wait on God and step out to "do our own thing" we must rely on our own fleshly sight, and this what the enemy wants.

The best way to see as a spiritual man is to "clean house" with confession and repentance. By turning our failings and sins over to the Lord with a humble and broken spirit, we are clearing the garbage away so we can "see" with the eyes of God. The more we do these acts of humility the clearer our spiritual sight will be, and the more secure our perimeter will be to keep the enemy out.

TDR) Training/Discussion Routine:

1. Discuss/confess/repent/absolve the areas where we each let the enemy have access to us through drugs, prostitution, rituals, etc.
2. Pray for healing and deliverance in these areas.

Week 8

Week 8

Your Mission — A Soldier's Authority

Many Christian soldiers are under the belief that individual Christians like you and I were never empowered by God to engage demons in combat. I have heard quite a few say things like, "Well, as long as I keep my eyes on Jesus I never have to confront demons. He will confront them for me." This is a nice thought, but not too scriptural. Keeping our eyes on Jesus is definitely scriptural, but so are His orders for us to use His authority to face demons in combat!

I have also heard some brothers and sisters mention that Jesus only gave authority to the twelve disciples to cast out demons and conduct spiritual warfare on His behalf. This is not true. He has given all of us the authority to do spiritual warfare in His name, all the time!

Let's look at the Word of God to see evidence of our authority in doing spiritual warfare:

Luke 10:17 says, *"And the seventy returned with joy, saying, 'Lord, even the demons are subject to us in Your Name.'"*

Jesus had commissioned seventy other believers (just ordinary ones like you and I) at the beginning of Luke 10 to go out ahead of Him and prepare the people for ministry. He sent them in pairs. In verse 17 they returned to Him and gave a report. He (Jesus) then affirms them in verse 19, *"Behold, I have given you authority to tread upon serpents and scorpions, and over all the power of the enemy, and nothing shall injure you."*

We all, to this day, have the same God-given authority to do face-to-face warfare with satanic forces that the saints had centuries ago. To say anything different is anti-Christ and whispered rumors from the enemy's camp.

It is important to know about your authority from God before you can walk in the commission He has given you. And that commission is spelled out clearly in Acts 26:16-18:

"...But rise and stand on your feet; for I have appeared to you, to appoint you a minister and a witness both of the things which you have seen, and of the things I will reveal to you. I will deliver you from the Jewish people, as well as from the Gentiles, to whom I now send you, to open their eyes, and turn them from darkness to light and from the power of Satan to God, that they may receive forgiveness of sins and an inheritance among them that are sanctified by faith in me."

TDR) Training/Discussion Routine:

1. What authority do you have in the spiritual war we fight each day?
2. What happens when you assert your own "authority" in warfare?
3. Why did Jesus send His soldiers (disciples) out two at a time? Why not by themselves?

Finale—Our Mission

"The Spirit of the Lord God is upon me, because the Lord has anointed me to preach good tidings to the poor. He has sent me to heal the brokenhearted, to proclaim liberty to the captives, and the opening of the prison to those who are bound; to proclaim the acceptable year of the Lord, and the day of vengeance of our God, to comfort all who mourn, to console those who mourn in Zion, to give them beauty for ashes, the oil of joy for mourning, the garment of praise for the spirit of heaviness, the planting of the Lord, that he may be glorified" Isaiah 61:1-3.

Full-color prints of the entire Norm Bergsma
Vietnam Collection can be obtained from:

In-Country Art
1306 2nd St.
Kirkland, WA 98033
425-827-0850

Visit the In-Country Art Website:
www.geocities.com/in-countryart/

Point Man International Ministries

Headquarters
P.O. Box 267
Springbrook, NY 14140
e-mail: danausmc@earthlink.net

Emergency hotline for veterans: 1-800-877-
VETS

To order additional copies of this call the Point
Man Book Bunker: 1-517-584-6201

Or write:
Point Man Book Bunker
P.O. Box 627
Carson City, MI 48811

To order additional copies of

AFTER THE AMBUSH

have your credit card ready and call

(800) 917-BOOK

or send $8.99 plus $3.95 shipping and handling to

Books, Etc.
P. O. Box 1973
Albany, OR 97321

For more information on Chuck Dean's other publications visit his website at www.namvetbook.com